ADHD AFTER DIAGNOSIS

A Roadmap for Understanding Your Brain

TYLER MITCHELL

ADHD After Diagnosis:

A Roadmap for Understanding Your Brain

Copyright © 2025 by Tyler Mitchell

This book is not intended as a substitute for the medical advice of physicians or mental health professionals. The reader should regularly consult a physician or mental health professional in matters relating to health and particularly with respect to any symptoms that may require diagnosis or medical attention.

First Edition

ISBN: 979-8-9997272-0-6

For more resources and tools, visit: tylermitchell.com

DEDICATION

For everyone who's ever wondered "What's wrong with me?" when the real question was "What do I need?"

And for my kids, who taught me that different isn't broken—it's just different.

Table of Contents

Introduction: The Thing Nobody Tells You After Diagnosis

When I got my ADHD diagnosis in my 40s, I thought I'd finally found the missing piece of the puzzle.

I expected relief. Understanding. Maybe even some kind of roadmap for what comes next.

Instead, I got... more questions.

"Okay, so now what? Do I take medication? Do I tell people? How do I explain 40 years of thinking I was just bad at life? And why does knowing I have ADHD somehow make me feel more broken, not less?"

If you're reading this, you might be in that same weird space. You finally have an answer to why things have felt so hard. But instead of feeling fixed, you might feel more confused than ever.

That's not failure. That's normal.

Getting diagnosed is just the beginning. The real work, the good work, is figuring out how to live with this new understanding of who you've always been.

What This Book Actually Is

This isn't a medical guide. I'm a strategy consultant by day (don't ask me what that means because I still can't explain it clearly), and I'm definitely not qualified to give medical advice.

This is a guide for the emotional and practical journey that happens after diagnosis. It's about understanding what ADHD actually means, reframing your past without erasing it, building systems that work with your brain, deciding when and how to share your diagnosis, and creating a life that feels sustainable.

I wrote this from the perspective of someone who's been where you are. Who's felt the shame, the confusion, the weird grief that comes with realizing you've been running a different operating system your whole life.

But I also wrote it from the perspective of someone who's made it through to the other side. Who's learned to work with their brain instead of against it. Who's stopped apologizing for being wired differently.

And who's discovered that when you start understanding and accepting yourself, something beautiful happens: it ripples out to everyone around you.

How This Book Works

Here's what I learned about ADHD brains and learning: many of us need to consume information differently than traditional guides expect.

Most self-help books assume you'll read a chapter, do the exercises, then move on. But if you're like me, you need to read through everything first to get the big picture, then go back and do the deeper work.

So this book is designed to work with your brain:

Read through the entire book first to understand the full framework, then go back to work with the reflection questions when you're ready.

You don't have to do this in order. You don't have to answer every question. You don't have to finish it in a certain timeframe.

Your brain works differently, and this book respects that.

A Note About Perfection

I'm going to say this now because I know how many ADHD brains work: **You don't have to do this perfectly.**

You don't have to answer every reflection question. You don't have to have profound insights in every section. You don't have to finish the whole book before you start seeing benefits.

This is about progress, not perfection. About understanding, not optimization.

If you read one chapter and it clicks something into place, that's enough. If you skip three chapters and dive deep into the one that speaks to you, that's also enough.

Your healing doesn't have to look like anyone else's.

You're Not Starting Over

Before we begin, I want to be clear about something: **You're not starting over. You're starting with context.**

All those years you thought you were failing? You were actually adapting. Surviving. Learning to navigate a world that wasn't designed for how your brain works.

You weren't broken. You were just missing the manual.

This book is that manual. Written by someone who's been there, for people who are figuring it out as they go.

You're not behind. You're not too late. You're exactly where you need to be.

Let's begin.

Chapter 1: You're Not Broken, You're Wired Differently

Why ADHD isn't a failure of discipline (it's a difference in design)

Instead of asking 'why can't I focus?' I've started asking 'what do I need to tweak to keep going?

@tylercmitchell

The Path to Understanding

We homeschool our five kids, and my wife kept bringing up concerns about our oldest son. He'd pace while doing schoolwork, had trouble focusing, would get overwhelmed by things that seemed simple. And every single time, I'd dismiss her concerns with the same response: "I was just like that as a kid. Don't worry about it. He'll be fine."

I said this for *years*. Looking back, it's almost comical how many conversations ended with me waving off her concerns because "I turned out just fine."

Everything changed when she accidentally left a book about child development running during the section on autism and ADHD. She came to me saying, "They're describing our son."

As we started researching both autism and ADHD for our son, I began recognizing myself in many of the descriptions. While I saw similarities with both conditions, ADHD seemed to match what was affecting me most directly.

When I called my brother (who's an occupational therapist working with neurodivergent kids) to get his thoughts on our son's potential needs, he went quiet for a moment.

Then he said, "I've actually thought your son was on the spectrum for quite a while."

"Why haven't you said anything before?" I asked.

"I've seen families torn apart by this news, and I didn't want that to get in the way of our relationship."

While we continued the assessment process for our son (who did receive both ASD and ADHD diagnoses), I reached out to a couple of coworkers I knew had ADHD, asking about the process of getting diagnosed as an adult.

Both of them (separately, people who didn't know each other) said the exact same thing: "You're just now figuring out you're ADHD? I've known for years."

I was stunned. "What are you talking about? I'm not hyperactive. I'm pretty organized. I don't forget things."

"You've just built systems to compensate," one of them said.

And that's when it hit me.

The Systems I Didn't Know I Was Building

I *did* have systems for everything. Rigid ones. I'd tell new coworkers, "Here's how I work. If you have a better way, I'm willing to adapt, but otherwise, let's stick to this approach." I thought I was being organized and professional.

What I was actually doing was creating accommodations for a brain I didn't understand yet.

I'd developed elaborate routines because I inherently knew I could get thrown off by disruptions. I'd insist on written follow-ups after meetings because I knew I might miss important details in verbal conversations. I'd block out extra time for tasks because I'd learned the hard way that my time estimates were usually wrong.

For decades, I'd been unconsciously adapting to my ADHD brain while telling myself I was just being thorough.

Reflection: What systems or routines have you built that you now realize might have been accommodations?

What I Thought It Was

Before I had the ADHD language, I had a lot of labels I gave myself.

I thought I was someone who needed more structure than most people. Someone who got overwhelmed by too many variables. Someone who worked better alone because I could control my environment.

I didn't think these were flaws, exactly, but I definitely thought they were quirks I needed to manage around.

The worst part? When I couldn't make my systems work, when life got too chaotic or unpredictable, I thought it was a personal failing. Like I wasn't disciplined enough or organized enough or just *enough*.

Reflection: What's something you've been blaming yourself for that makes more sense now?

What ADHD Really Is

Let's zoom out for a second and talk about what ADHD actually is, beyond the hyperactive kid stereotype.

ADHD isn't just about being easily distracted or bouncing off walls. **It's a regulation disorder.**

Regulating attention. Regulating emotion. Regulating energy, time, memory, motivation.

Most of us know what needs to happen. We just can't always get there. That gap between "I know" and "I did it" is the invisible struggle no one sees.

What that looks like in real life:

- You can hyperfocus for 8 hours on something random but can't start a task you actually care about
- You experience emotions intensely, both the good and the overwhelming
- You forget things you desperately want to remember
- You need pressure or urgency to activate, even for things that matter to you
- You're constantly rebuilding systems that worked until... they didn't

This isn't about intelligence. It's not about caring. It's about a brain that processes information, manages emotions, and directs attention differently than the world expects.

The Research Behind the Reframe

What the science tells us about ADHD that most people never hear:

ADHD is a disorder of executive function, not just attention.
Executive function is like the CEO of your brain. It manages
planning, prioritizing, initiating tasks, and switching between them.
When that system is inconsistent, everything else gets harder.

Emotional dysregulation is a core trait, not a side effect. For
decades, the emotional piece of ADHD was overlooked. But
researchers like Dr. Russell Barkley have shown that emotional
intensity and regulation challenges are central to the ADHD
experience.

Working memory issues play a major role. Working memory is
your brain's scratchpad. It holds information while you use it. When
it's glitchy, you might forget what you were doing mid-task, lose track
of multi-step instructions, or struggle to connect past experiences to
present decisions.

Time blindness is real. Many people with ADHD struggle with
time perception. Five minutes can feel like an hour when you're
bored, or three hours can disappear without notice when you're
focused.

This isn't just helpful information. It's validation. These aren't
character flaws. They're neurological differences.

Reflection: Complete this reframe:

- **Old thought:** "I'm just..."
- **New understanding:** "My brain...

The Reframe That Changes Everything

Instead of seeing your past as a series of failures, try seeing it as a
series of adaptations.

- You weren't lazy. You were conserving energy for the things that mattered most.
- You weren't scattered. You were managing competing priorities without a system to organize them.
- You weren't too emotional. You were feeling everything intensely in a world that rewards emotional suppression.
- You weren't inconsistent. You were working with a brain that operates in cycles, not straight lines.

This isn't about making excuses. It's about accuracy. It's about seeing your past and yourself with understanding instead of criticism.

What This Means Going Forward

Understanding that you're wired differently isn't just about the past. It's about the future.

It means you can stop trying to fit into systems that weren't designed for your brain. You can start building ones that are.

It means you can stop blaming yourself for struggling with things that genuinely are harder for you. And you can start finding tools and support that actually help.

It means you can stop hiding parts of yourself out of shame. And you can start showing up as who you actually are.

Most importantly, it means you can stop waiting to be "fixed" before you start living. Because you were never broken in the first place.

When my coworkers told me they'd known I was ADHD for years, my first instinct was embarrassment. How had I missed something so obvious to others?

But now I see it differently. They weren't seeing something wrong with me. They were recognizing someone else who'd learned to work with their brain in creative ways.

You're not broken. You never were. You're just finally getting the user manual for how you've always operated.

And that manual starts with one simple truth: different isn't wrong. It's just different.

Sidenote: ADHD rarely travels alone. If you're reading these descriptions thinking "Yes, but I also struggle with anxiety, depression, or other challenges," that's incredibly common. Getting one diagnosis often opens doors to understanding other pieces of the puzzle. You're not more complicated. You're getting a more complete map of how your brain works.

Key takeaways: You weren't failing all those years. You were adapting without a manual. The systems you built, the workarounds you created, the way you learned to survive? That wasn't evidence of being broken. That was evidence of being resilient.

Chapter 2: It's Not Just Distraction, It's Regulation

The hidden triad of attention, emotion, and energy

Let me guess. You've told yourself something like this before:

"I don't have a focus problem. I just can't control what I focus on."

You can lock in for 8 hours on something random but can't answer an email or start a task you care about.

I discovered this firsthand when I transitioned from my old job as an X-ray tech (where I was constantly moving around, helping patients, facing new situations every day) to my current role as a strategy consultant (and yes, I still can't explain what that means, but I have fun with it).

Suddenly, I was expected to sit at a desk and solve abstract problems. And that's when everything fell apart.

I'd be given an assignment and wouldn't know how to start. I wouldn't know how to get to the point where I could gain understanding on what I needed to do. So I'd do what felt most reasonable in the moment: I'd open YouTube and watch videos all day. Not about the topic I was supposed to be working on, mind you. Just videos. Anything to distract myself from the stress of not knowing where to begin.

This was pre-diagnosis, and it was part of what led me to getting assessed. Because I started getting really depressed. I'm the breadwinner for my family of seven, we'd just moved to a new city, and I was convinced I wouldn't be able to replace this income if I got fired. The pressure was enormous, but instead of helping me focus, it was paralyzing me completely.

That's not a focus deficit. That's focus dysregulation. Which is exactly what ADHD actually is.

Why This Feels So Hard

The tough part most people don't see: You can care deeply about something and still not be able to start. You can know what's urgent and still freeze. You can have good intentions and still crash after one disruption.

This isn't a character flaw. It's a regulation challenge.

When I started medication, my brain got quiet for the first time in my life. What I realized in that moment was profound: I hadn't known it wasn't normal to have multiple conversations running simultaneously in your head. But when those mental radio stations got turned down from five or six to maybe one or two, and the volume dropped significantly, I could finally step back and observe what had been happening.

I also hadn't realized it wasn't normal to wake up at 2 or 3 in the morning and start replaying every embarrassing moment from the past decades. I thought that was just what brains did, that it was part of processing experiences and learning from mistakes.

But when that mental noise reduced, I understood these weren't signs of a thoughtful, reflective mind. They were signs of a dysregulated system trying to manage more input than it could handle.

We Don't Need Focus. We Need Regulation.

That's what makes ADHD so frustrating and misunderstood. Because we can do hard things, just not consistently. Not because we're flaky or don't care enough. Because the system running in the background keeps glitching.

When I was undiagnosed, I thought this inconsistency was proof that I was undisciplined. That I didn't want success badly enough. That I was fundamentally broken.

But here's what I wish someone had told me: **You're not inconsistent. You're dysregulated.**

The Triangle That Explains Everything

If you remember one thing from this chapter, let it be this: ADHD isn't just about focus. It's about this triangle:

Attention. Emotion. Energy.

All three are constantly in play. When one is off, the others follow.

Here's what this cascade actually looks like in real life:

Emotional storm → Focus crashes: You get criticism from your boss about a missed deadline. That rejection sensitivity kicks in, flooding your working memory with shame and worry. Suddenly you can't concentrate on anything else, even though you have three other urgent tasks waiting.

Energy dip → Emotions spike: You've been pushing through a big project for days without proper breaks. Your regulation reserves are depleted. Now your teenager's normal attitude feels personally attacking, you snap over dishes in the sink, and you can't understand why everything feels so hard.

Task overwhelm → Emotional freeze → Energy drain: You look at your to-do list and it feels impossible. The overwhelm triggers shutdown mode, you can't think clearly about priorities, can't access your usual problem-solving, can't even decide where to start. So you scroll your phone for two hours, which makes you feel guilty, which drains you more.

See how they cascade? It's not three separate problems. It's one integrated system trying to regulate itself the only way it knows how.

Reflection: What have you been calling "distraction" that might actually be dysregulation?

What the Research Actually Says

This isn't just theory. Research backs this up, especially the work of Dr. Russell Barkley, who redefined ADHD not as an attention issue, but as a self-regulation disorder tied to executive function.

What the science shows:

Executive function is the real issue. Think of executive function as your brain's project manager. It handles planning, prioritizing, initiating tasks, and switching between them. When that system is inconsistent, everything else becomes harder.

Let me show you what inconsistent executive function looked like in my actual workday:

I'd start Monday with a clear plan: finish the client presentation, respond to emails, prep for Thursday's meeting. Simple enough.

But then I'd open my computer and see seventeen browser tabs from Friday's research rabbit hole. My executive function system had to decide: close them or keep them? Each tab represented a choice, and choices require mental energy.

Then an email would come in marked "urgent." My brain would have to switch contexts entirely from presentation mode to problem-solving mode. More executive function load.

By 11am, I'd made hundreds of micro-decisions I wasn't even conscious of, and my mental bandwidth was already strained. The important work I'd planned? It felt impossible, not because it was hard, but because my brain's management system was maxed out.

Emotional dysregulation is central, not secondary. For decades, the emotional piece of ADHD was overlooked. But research now shows that emotional intensity and regulation challenges are core features, not side effects.

Working memory crashes are common. Working memory is your brain's sticky note system. It holds information while you use it. When it's glitchy, you forget what you were doing mid-task, lose track of instructions, or struggle to connect past experiences to present decisions.

Time perception is genuinely different. Many people with ADHD struggle with time blindness. Five minutes can feel like an hour when you're understimulated, or three hours can disappear when you're hyperfocused.

This matters because it means the struggle is real. You're not imagining it. The invisible load you've been carrying has a name and a neurological basis.

The ADHD Iceberg

Imagine an iceberg. Above the surface, people see you:

- Zoning out during meetings
- Missing deadlines
- Not replying to texts
- Starting projects you don't finish

Below the surface, you're dealing with:

- Task paralysis when things feel too big or vague
- Emotional overwhelm that shuts down thinking
- Decision fatigue from managing too many variables
- Time blindness that makes planning feel impossible
- Working memory crashes that lose important details
- The constant internal conversations competing for attention

That's why ADHD is so often misunderstood. What people see is only a sliver of what's actually happening.

The Myth of "Just Try Harder"

Something that trips up a lot of people: ADHD doesn't mean you can't focus. It means you can't always control what you focus on.

You might hyperfocus on organizing your bookshelf when you have a deadline looming. Not because you don't care about the deadline, but because your attention regulation system is seeking the dopamine hit of completion, and organizing feels more immediately rewarding than the complex, ambiguous work task.

This is why "just try harder" doesn't work for many ADHD brains. We're often already trying incredibly hard. The issue isn't effort. It's that we're working against a system that's wired differently.

I remember a coworker once telling me, after I'd shared my diagnosis, "I don't get it. You're one of the hardest workers I know. You always seem so focused."

What he didn't see were the elaborate systems I'd built to create that appearance of focus. The way I'd block out twice as much time as I needed for tasks because I knew I'd get distracted. The detailed notes I'd take in meetings because I couldn't trust my working memory. The way I'd arrive early and stay late to compensate for the productivity I lost during the day to internal wrestling matches.

I wasn't naturally focused. I was compensation-focused.

When Focus Feels Effortless

But there's an interesting part: there are times when focus feels easy. When you're in flow, when you're hyperfocused, when everything clicks.

For me, focus feels effortless when:

- There's an immediate deadline
- I'm emotionally regulated (not stressed, anxious, or overwhelmed)
- I'm well-rested and not fighting basic needs
- The task matches my interest level or feels meaningful
- I'm not juggling competing priorities or distractions

These aren't accidents. They're clues about how my regulation system works best.

On the flip side, focus tends to fall apart when:

- The task is vague, overwhelming, or has unclear parameters
- I'm emotionally activated (stressed, anxious, or hurt)

- I'm physically depleted (tired, hungry, or overstimulated)
- There's no external urgency, deadline, or accountability
- I'm trying to manage too many competing priorities at once

Again, these aren't personal failings. They're system overloads.

Reflection: When does focus feel effortless for you? What conditions are present? When does focus fall apart? What patterns do you notice?

The Regulation Reframe

The shift that changes everything: stop thinking of ADHD as a focus problem. Start thinking of it as a regulation problem.

Instead of asking "Why can't I focus?" ask "What's my regulation system trying to tell me?"

- If you're avoiding a task, maybe it's too big and needs to be broken down
- If you're hyperfocusing on the wrong thing, maybe you need a dopamine hit before tackling the harder task
- If you're emotionally activated, maybe you need to address the feeling before you can think clearly
- If you're exhausted, maybe you need rest, not more productivity strategies

This reframe takes you from self-criticism to self-advocacy. From fighting your brain to working with it.

What This Means Going Forward

Understanding that ADHD is about regulation, not just attention, changes how you approach everything.

It means you can stop blaming yourself for being "distractible" and start building systems that support regulation.

It means you can stop trying to force focus and start creating conditions where focus feels more natural.

It means you can stop seeing your struggles as personal failings and start seeing them as information about what your brain needs.

Most importantly, it means you can stop fighting yourself and start working with the system you actually have.

The goal isn't to eliminate the mental conversations entirely (sometimes they're playing useful information). The goal is to turn down the volume enough that you can choose which conversation to listen to.

Reflection: What's one way you can work with your regulation system instead of against it?

Sidenote: The regulation challenges we're talking about can look a lot like anxiety disorders, depression, or autism traits. That's because they often occur together. If these descriptions resonate but don't feel like the complete picture, trust that instinct. Many people discover ADHD as part of understanding a broader neurodivergent profile.

Key takeaways: ADHD isn't about lacking focus. It's about not being able to control where your focus goes. When you understand the attention-emotion-energy triangle, you can stop fighting your brain and start working with your actual operating system.

Chapter 3: The Patterns Start to Click

You're not random. You're running a system you didn't know existed.

The hardest part of change? Not knowing where to start, so you don't start at all.

@tylercmitchell

If I could go back and tell my past self ten years before I was diagnosed, it would be this:

"You're not scattered. You're stuck in a loop you couldn't see."

Not broken. Not lazy. Not doomed to rebuild your whole life every Sunday night. Just running a system you didn't know was running.

And once you start to see those loops? It changes everything.

You realize: "Oh... I've done this before. I always do this after a big deadline." Or: "Yep, I'm in the part where I pretend to start fresh, then crash again by Thursday."

For me, one of the first patterns I recognized was what happened after I'd meet a major deadline or finish an intense project. I'd work incredibly hard, hyperfocus for days, push through on minimal sleep, get everything done. And then I'd completely fall apart for the next week.

I used to think this was just me being weak or undisciplined. I'd beat myself up about it: "Why can't I maintain momentum? Why do I always crash right when I should be building on success?"

But then I started noticing: this happened every single time. Without fail. After every major push, there was a corresponding crash.

That's when I realized: this wasn't random. This wasn't a character flaw. This was my brain's way of recovering from intense focus periods. The crash wasn't a bug. It was a feature.

Once I saw that pattern, I could plan for it. I could build recovery time into my schedule. I could stop fighting the crash and start working with it.

And the moment that pattern clicked into place? It was like someone handed me a decoder ring to my own life.

The Thing About ADHD Patterns

Here's what I wish someone had told me: **You're not inconsistent. You're cyclical.**

Many ADHD brains don't operate in straight lines. We operate in loops, spirals, and waves. And because the world expects linear progress, we've learned to see our natural rhythms as failures.

But they're not failures. They're patterns. And patterns can be understood, predicted, and eventually redirected.

Remember how executive function inconsistency makes patterns hard to see while you're in them? Here's what that looks like:

We rebuild instead of repeat. Every time something breaks, we go, "Well, guess that didn't work," and we reinvent everything from scratch. This keeps us from seeing the pattern under the disruption.

I Didn't Realize I Had Patterns

For years, I thought I was just bad at life. Really bad at life.

I'd watch other people seem to glide through their days with some kind of internal GPS, while I felt like I was constantly getting lost in my own neighborhood.

I didn't realize that my "getting lost" followed a predictable route. I had no idea that my crashes, my restarts, my cycles of enthusiasm and burnout were actually following an internal logic.

Some loops I eventually recognized:

The Amazon Delivery Loop: Feel understimulated or stressed → Start browsing online for something new → Get excited about a potential hobby or tool → Order multiple items → Feel guilty about spending → Use guilt as motivation to be productive → Get overwhelmed by productivity pressure → Feel understimulated again → Repeat.

I literally had weeks where Amazon delivered to my house five times. My family would joke about it, but underneath I was mortified. What was wrong with me? Why couldn't I stop buying things I didn't need?

Once I recognized this as a dopamine-seeking pattern triggered by stress or boredom, I could start addressing the underlying need instead of just the symptom.

The Perfect System Paradox: Get frustrated with current productivity approach → Research the "perfect" system → Get excited and reorganize everything → System works great for 3-7 days → System starts feeling restrictive or boring → Abandon system → Feel like a failure → Start researching new systems → Repeat.

I had so many abandoned planners, apps, and organizational methods. Each time I'd think, "This is it! This is the system that will finally work!" And each time I'd end up back at square one, convinced I was just fundamentally bad at being organized.

The Social Energy Crash: Accept social invitation while feeling good → Look forward to event → Day of event, feel overwhelmed but push through → Have genuinely good time at event → Come home completely drained → Need 2-3 days of isolation to recover → Feel guilty about being antisocial → Force myself to be more social → Repeat.

This one was particularly confusing because I genuinely enjoy people and social activities. But I couldn't understand why something I enjoyed would leave me feeling so depleted, or why I'd need so much recovery time afterward.

These were my personal patterns, but every ADHD brain has its own version. You might recognize the Overcommit Cycle, the Perfectionism Paralysis, the Dopamine Chase, or the Emotional Shutdown loop. The specific content doesn't matter as much as learning to recognize when you're in a familiar cycle instead of a random crisis.

Reflection: What's a pattern that keeps happening in your life?

Why Patterns Feel Invisible

There's a reason these loops stayed hidden for so long. Many ADHD brains are wired in ways that make pattern recognition challenging:

We live in the emotional present. When you're in the middle of a shame spiral, it feels like the first time you've ever been there. The emotional intensity drowns out the memory of previous similar experiences.

We focus on content, not context. We get caught up in what went wrong (the specific purchase, the particular social event) instead of noticing the when, where, and how it happened.

We're rebuilding constantly. Instead of tweaking systems, we tend to scrap them and start over. This prevents us from seeing what actually worked and what didn't.

We blame ourselves, not the system. When something breaks down, we assume it's a personal failing rather than a system design issue.

The Moment Things Click

But once you start to see one pattern, you start to see them all.

It's like those magic eye pictures. You stare and stare, and then suddenly the hidden image pops out, and you can't unsee it.

I discovered this firsthand when I helped a coworker who was struggling with deadlines. Once we understood his ADHD and set up a simple body doubling session, he knocked out weeks of backlogged work in a single afternoon. (I'll share the full story of how that worked in Chapter 8.)

That's when I really understood: this wasn't about willpower or caring or intelligence. This was about understanding the system and working with it instead of against it.

Reflection: Think of a recent challenge. Can you map it out?

- What triggered it:
- How did you feel:
- What did you do:
- What might have helped instead:

The Pattern Behind the Pattern

What's fascinating: most ADHD loops aren't actually about the surface issue. They're about regulation.

When you map your patterns, you'll often discover that:

- The "productivity" loop is actually about managing energy
- The "perfectionism" loop is actually about managing anxiety
- The "overcommit" loop is actually about managing dopamine and social connection
- The "shutdown" loop is actually about managing overwhelm

This is why surface-level solutions don't work. You can't solve an energy management problem with a new planner. You can't solve an anxiety management problem with better goal-setting.

You have to address the regulation issue underneath.

Your Patterns Are Information

Once you start to see your patterns, it's tempting to judge them. To see them as things you need to fix or eliminate.

But here's a different way to think about it: **Your patterns are information.** They're your brain's way of trying to solve problems you didn't know you had.

The Amazon delivery loop? That's your brain trying to manage understimulation and the dopamine deficit that comes with boring or stressful tasks.

The perfectionism paralysis? That's your brain trying to manage anxiety about judgment and rejection.

The social energy crash? That's your brain trying to balance your need for connection with your limited processing capacity.

These aren't broken responses. They're adaptive responses that may have outlived their usefulness.

What Changes When You See the Pattern

When you recognize a loop while you're in it, something shifts. Instead of feeling like you're failing again, you can think, "Oh, this is one of those times."

You're not stuck. You're in a familiar place. And familiar places can be navigated.

You might not be able to exit the loop immediately. But you can slow it down. You can catch it earlier next time. You can build in circuit breakers.

Most importantly, you can stop blaming yourself for being in the loop and start getting curious about what the loop is trying to tell you.

For example, when I notice I'm browsing Amazon for the third time in a day, instead of beating myself up about it, I can ask: "What am I actually looking for right now? What need am I trying to meet? Am I bored? Stressed? Avoiding something?"

Sometimes the answer is that I need a break. Sometimes it's that I need to tackle a task I've been putting off. Sometimes it's that I need to move my body or change my environment.

The shopping impulse is just the messenger. The real information is in what triggered it.

Building Pattern Awareness

Pattern recognition is a skill. Like any skill, it gets better with practice.

Start small. Pick one area of your life where you notice recurring challenges. Maybe it's morning routines. Maybe it's work transitions. Maybe it's social situations.

For the next week, just observe. Don't try to change anything. Just notice:

- What triggers the pattern?
- What emotions come up?
- What do you typically do?
- How does it usually resolve?

You're not looking for solutions yet. You're just gathering data.

I keep a note in my phone where I jot down patterns as I notice them. Not to judge them, just to track them. "Stayed up too late researching X when I should have been sleeping." "Felt overwhelmed by Y and shut down instead of asking for help." "Got hyperfocused on Z and forgot to eat lunch."

Over time, these notes reveal the invisible architecture of how my brain operates. And once you can see the architecture, you can start making intentional modifications instead of just hoping things will be different next time.

Reflection: What might one of your patterns be trying to tell you about what you need?

The Relief of Recognition

There's a particular kind of relief that comes with recognizing your patterns. It's the relief of moving from "What's wrong with me?" to "Oh, this is how I work."

You're not random. You're not unpredictable. You're not fundamentally flawed.

You're running a complex system that's been trying to take care of you, often without your conscious input. And now that you can see how it works, you can start being an active participant in your own life instead of just a confused observer.

But there's one more pattern that took me longer to recognize, the biggest one of all. It's not just individual loops. It's the way ADHD energy itself moves in predictable cycles between intense focus and complete exhaustion. Once I understood this rhythm, everything else started to make sense.

Key takeaways: You're not random or unpredictable. You're running patterns you couldn't see. Once you start recognizing your loops, you can slow them down, catch them earlier, and build in circuit breakers. Your patterns aren't problems to eliminate. They're information about what you need.

Chapter 4: The ADHD Pendulum

Why you swing between "on fire" and "burned out," and what to do about it

IT WASN'T A FLOW OF EXPECTATIONS I WAS MANAGING. IT WAS A PILEUP. AND SOMEHOW, IT HAD ALL LANDED ON ME.

@tylercmitchell

Remember that Amazon delivery loop from Chapter 3? What I didn't understand then was that it wasn't just a random pattern. It was my pendulum in action, swinging between understimulation and overstimulation, between "crushing it" and "can't even function."

And if you have ADHD, you probably have your own version of this swing.

Let me ask you something: Do you have two modes? "Crushing it" and "can't even reply to a text"?

If you're nodding, you're not alone. Welcome to what I call the ADHD Pendulum.

It's that feeling of going from superhuman productivity to complete shutdown, often with zero warning. One day you're on fire, handling everything, feeling like you've finally figured it out. The next day, you can barely get out of bed, and simple tasks feel impossible.

Here's what I wish someone had told me: This isn't inconsistency. It's your brain trying to regulate itself the only way it knows how.

What the Pendulum Feels Like

"I go from on fire to burned out, and I never see it coming."

That's how someone described it to me recently, and it perfectly captures the whiplash of ADHD energy management.

What the swing looks like:

On fire mode: You're saying yes to everything. You have three new projects, you're sending emails at 2am, you're reorganizing your entire life system. You feel alive, productive, unstoppable. You're convinced you've finally figured out how to adult properly.

Burnout mode: Decision fatigue hits like a wall. You're avoiding your phone, snapping at people you love, and can't even choose what to eat for lunch. Everything feels too hard. The idea of making one more decision makes you want to cry.

Ghost mode: You disappear. Stop responding to messages, avoid commitments, retreat into Netflix or scrolling. You know you're behind, but you can't make yourself engage. The thought of facing your responsibilities feels overwhelming.

And then, just when you think you'll never feel motivated again, something flips. You're back in "on fire" mode, wondering why you ever struggled.

Reflection: What's one way the "pendulum" shows up in your life?

Why This Happens

There's actual neuroscience behind this pendulum swing. It's not a character flaw or a willpower problem. It's how many ADHD brains handle energy and dopamine regulation.

Dopamine-driven interest spikes: When something lights up your ADHD brain, dopamine floods your system. You lock in. You hyperfocus. You're unstoppable. But this surge isn't self-regulating. There's no internal voice saying, "Hey, maybe take a break." You ride the wave until it crashes.

Poor interoception: This is your ability to sense internal cues, like hunger, fatigue, or overwhelm. Many people with ADHD have spotty interoception. We don't feel the buildup of burnout. We don't notice we're tired. We don't catch the edge of overwhelm until we're already over it.

Executive function crashes: After intense focus or output, your brain's executive function system needs recovery time. But we often don't recognize this need, so we keep pushing until the system essentially forces a shutdown.

Emotional memory of failure: When we do crash, we feel terrible about it. We promise ourselves we'll be different next time. This creates pressure to perform even harder when we're back in "on fire" mode, which sets us up for an even bigger crash.

It's a cycle that feeds itself.

My Personal Pendulum Story

Let me tell you about one of my most dramatic pendulum swings.

I'd just started posting about ADHD on social media, and one of my videos unexpectedly went viral. Suddenly, I had thousands of new followers, hundreds of comments, and messages pouring in from people saying my content was helping them.

I was *on fire*. I started creating content every day, responding to every comment, planning new projects. I was staying up until 2am making videos, waking up early to engage with comments. I felt like I was finally doing something meaningful with my life.

For about two weeks, I was Superman. I was balancing my full-time job, creating content, being present for my family, and still finding energy for new ideas.

And then I hit the wall.

It started with small things. I'd stare at my phone, knowing I should respond to messages, but feeling completely overwhelmed by the thought of crafting thoughtful replies. Then I stopped checking comments altogether. Then I stopped posting.

I went from creating daily content to radio silence. From feeling like I had endless energy to barely being able to handle my regular job responsibilities.

The shame spiral was intense. "You finally had momentum and you blew it. People were counting on you and you disappeared. You're not cut out for this."

It took me weeks to understand what had actually happened. I hadn't failed. I hadn't lost motivation. I'd burned through my regulation reserves and my brain had forced a recovery period.

The Pendulum Loop

Let me walk you through the typical progression:

Phase 1: Excitement/Activation You're fueled by a new idea, a surge of motivation, or a looming deadline. Everything feels possible. You're making plans, starting projects, saying yes to opportunities. The dopamine is flowing and you feel unstoppable.

Phase 2: Overload You stack too much on your plate. You're running on adrenaline and dopamine, but you don't feel it yet. Your brain is starting to strain under the load, but the warning signs are subtle. You might notice you're more irritable, making more mistakes, or feeling more scattered, but you push through.

Phase 3: The Crash Suddenly, everything feels hard. You stop. You hide. You shut down. Tasks that were easy yesterday feel impossible today. You can't understand what changed. The idea of tackling your to-do list makes you want to crawl under a blanket.

Phase 4: Guilt and Shame You start feeling bad about dropping the ball. You're frustrated with yourself. You might isolate or avoid the people and responsibilities you've been neglecting. "What's wrong with me? Why can't I just keep going like everyone else?"

Phase 5: Restart (Too Hard) You try to get back on track, but you overshoot. Instead of easing back in, you create new ambitious plans. You're determined to make up for lost time, which sets you up for another crash.

Phase 6: Repeat Back to excitement and overload. The cycle continues.

Reflection: What does your "on fire" mode look like? What are the warning signs it's becoming unsustainable?

What "On Fire" Really Looks Like

It's important to recognize your personal version of "on fire" mode because it often feels so good that we don't see it as unsustainable.

My "on fire" mode looked like:

- Saying yes to every interesting opportunity that came my way
- Starting multiple content projects simultaneously
- Working late into the night because I was "in the zone"
- Reorganizing my entire productivity system (again)
- Having brilliant ideas at 2am and then staying up to implement them
- Feeling like I could handle anything
- Buying tools and resources for all my new projects (hello, Amazon deliveries)

This mode feels amazing in the moment. But it's often your brain running on borrowed energy.

Looking back, I can see the warning signs I missed:

- Irritability when interrupted
- Forgetting to eat or drink water
- Difficulty transitioning between tasks
- Making more typos and small mistakes
- Feeling wired but tired
- Social interactions feeling more draining than usual

The Burnout Warning Signs

The tricky thing about ADHD burnout is that it doesn't announce itself. It creeps up slowly, then hits all at once.

Some early warning signs that you're tipping from momentum into overwhelm:

Decision fatigue: Simple choices become overwhelming. What to eat, what to wear, which email to answer first. Everything feels like a major decision that requires energy you don't have.

Emotional reactivity: You're snapping at people, feeling irritated by normal sounds, or crying at commercials. Your emotional regulation system is overloaded and everything feels more intense.

Avoidance behaviors: You're putting off phone calls, avoiding your inbox, or procrastinating on tasks that are normally easy for you. Your brain is trying to protect you from additional cognitive load.

Physical symptoms: Headaches, tension, changes in sleep or appetite. Your body is trying to tell you something but you're not listening.

Time distortion: Everything feels urgent and nothing feels urgent at the same time. You can't prioritize because everything seems equally important or equally pointless.

The challenge is that when you're in "on fire" mode, these warning signs are easy to dismiss. You tell yourself you're just busy, just stressed, just pushing through.

Reflection: What are your burnout warning signs? When do you first notice you're tipping into overwhelm?

Finding Your Reset Anchors

The goal isn't to eliminate the pendulum swing. That's like trying to stop the ocean from having tides. The goal is to catch the swing earlier and have tools to bring yourself back to center.

I call these tools "reset anchors." They're small, concrete actions that help you regulate when you notice you're swinging too far in either direction.

Physical reset anchors:

- A 20-minute walk with no destination (this is my go-to)
- A hot shower or bath

- Stretching or light movement
- Deep breathing or brief meditation

Cognitive reset anchors:

- Writing down three things you're grateful for
- Doing a "brain dump" of everything you're thinking about
- Reviewing your actual priorities (not your ambitious ones)
- Asking yourself: "What would I do if I only had energy for one thing?"

Social reset anchors:

- Texting a friend: "I'm spiraling a bit, just wanted to check in"
- Asking for help with one specific thing
- Saying no to one commitment
- Having an honest conversation about your capacity

Environmental reset anchors:

- Cleaning one small space
- Lighting a candle or changing the lighting
- Playing calming music
- Removing visual clutter from your workspace

The key is to identify your reset anchors before you need them. When you're in the middle of a swing, decision-making becomes much harder.

To find your personal reset anchors, pay attention this week to what naturally helps when you're struggling. Not what you think should help, but what actually does help. Keep a simple note: "Felt overwhelmed at 2pm, took a walk, felt better." That's data about your reset system.

Your anchors might be completely different from mine. Maybe cold showers wake you up but walks make you more scattered. Maybe tidying calms you but music overstimulates you. There's no right answer, only what works for your specific nervous system.

Working With the Pendulum

Once you understand your pendulum pattern, you can start to work with it instead of against it.

When you're in "on fire" mode:

- Celebrate it, but don't overcommit to future-you
- Build in recovery time after intense periods
- Check in with your body and emotional state regularly
- Remember that this energy isn't infinite
- Use this time for your most important work, not your most extensive to-do list

When you're in burnout mode:

- Don't fight it. Rest is productive.
- Focus on basics: sleep, food, gentle movement
- Avoid making major decisions or commitments
- Remind yourself this is temporary
- Lower your expectations to match your actual capacity

When you're in ghost mode:

- Start very small. One text. One task. One step.
- Don't try to make up for lost time all at once
- Reach out for connection, even if it feels hard
- Be kind to yourself about the retreat
- Remember that hiding is often your brain's way of protection

---

Reflection: What's one reset anchor you could try when you notice you're swinging too far in either direction?

You Don't Have to Live in Extremes

The pendulum swing is natural for many people with ADHD. But you don't have to live in constant extremes.

With awareness and the right tools, you can:

- Catch the swing earlier
- Make the swings less dramatic
- Recover more quickly
- Build more sustainable rhythms

The goal isn't to eliminate your natural energy cycles. It's to work with them more consciously.

A Different Way to Think About Consistency

The world rewards linear consistency. But many people with ADHD are cyclical. We have seasons of high energy and seasons of recovery.

Instead of fighting this, what if you planned for it?

What if you scheduled challenging projects during your high-energy seasons and protected your recovery seasons?

What if you measured success not by daily consistency, but by overall rhythm and sustainability?

What if you stopped apologizing for having natural cycles and started honoring them?

This isn't about lowering standards. It's about working with your actual operating system instead of trying to force it into someone else's mold.

The Pendulum Is a Feature, Not a Bug

I used to think the pendulum swing was evidence that I was broken. That I wasn't cut out for sustained success or reliable performance.

But I've come to see it differently. The pendulum swing is actually one of the strengths of many ADHD brains. It allows us to have periods of intense focus and creativity that neurotypical brains can't sustain.

The key is learning to surf the wave instead of being crushed by it.

When you understand your pendulum pattern, you can:

- Harness high-energy periods for your most important work
- Use your recovery periods for reflection and planning
- Build sustainable systems that account for natural rhythms
- Stop fighting yourself and start working with yourself

You're not inconsistent. You're cyclical. And there's tremendous power in understanding and working with your natural cycles.

Now when Amazon shows up at my house multiple times in one week, I don't just feel shame about the spending. I see it as information. My brain is seeking stimulation or trying to solve a problem. Instead of judging the symptom, I can get curious about the underlying need.

Sometimes that means I need a more engaging project. Sometimes it means I need to address a source of stress. Sometimes it means I need to acknowledge that I'm in a low-energy period and need different kinds of support.

The deliveries aren't the problem. They're the messenger.

Key takeaways: The swing between "on fire" and "burned out" isn't inconsistency. It's how ADHD brains naturally cycle through energy and regulation. Instead of fighting the pendulum, learn to work with it: harness high-energy periods for important work, protect recovery time, and catch the swing earlier with reset anchors.

Chapter 5: Reframing the Shame

How to stop punishing yourself for struggling

Let's just start here, because this was one of the most consistent thoughts in my head for most of my life:

"What is wrong with me?"

And not in a joking way. I mean the quiet, gut-punch kind of way. The kind that hits you after you miss a deadline you swore you'd remember, or snap at someone you care about for something small, or forget the one thing you were trying so hard to remember.

I used to say that to myself almost daily. And not out loud, just quietly. Like a background hum.

"What's wrong with me?"

Most people didn't see what I was actually wrestling with. They didn't see the fifteen mental post-it notes I was juggling to try and leave the house on time. They didn't see the cascade of panic behind a missed calendar alert. They just saw the late reply. The ghosted message. The dropped ball.

And because they didn't see it, I started to believe their version of the story.

"I must just be careless." "I must not care enough." "I'm the problem."

And I carried that. For years.

The Quiet Damage

This is the quiet damage that ADHD can do. Not just in the tasks we drop, but in the stories we start to tell ourselves about what those drops mean.

That's where shame comes in.

ADHD shame doesn't come from being lazy. It comes from being told over and over, sometimes with words, sometimes with just a sigh or a look, that our struggles were moral failures. That we should've done better.

And after a while? We start to believe it.

I've seen this most clearly as a parent. There was this moment with my son. He'd made a small mistake, something super normal, and I watched him absolutely unravel over it. I could see it in his body. The shame. The belief that he had failed as a person.

And it hit me so hard, because I realized: He was repeating the same things I used to say to myself. Word for word.

"I always mess this up." "What's wrong with me?" "Why can't I just do it right?"

That wasn't just a bad moment. That was inherited shame. That was taught.

Not because anyone meant to do harm, but because nobody gave us a better script. Nobody explained that what looked like "flaky" or "rude" or "immature" was actually a brain working overtime to regulate.

The Rejection Sensitivity Breakthrough

Remember when I mentioned those intense reactions to criticism that kept me up at night? A few months after diagnosis, I finally found the name for what I'd been experiencing my whole life: rejection sensitive dysphoria (RSD).

I'm not exaggerating when I say I started crying while reading about it. Real tears, not just getting misty-eyed. Because suddenly, decades of experiences finally had a name.

All those times when a small criticism would send me into a spiral that lasted for days. All those interactions where I'd replay a conversation over and over, convinced the other person thought I was incompetent or annoying. All those sleepless nights at 2 or 3 in the morning, running through every embarrassing thing I'd done since I was eight years old.

I used to tell my wife about these episodes: "I don't know what's wrong with me. I know logically that conversation wasn't a big deal. I know they probably didn't mean anything by their tone. But I can't stop thinking about it. I want to punch something, and I'm not a violent person."

Reading about RSD, I learned that this wasn't me being "too sensitive" or "dramatic." This was a neurological pattern tied to ADHD, where rejection (real or perceived) gets processed as genuine danger.

My brain had been treating every small slight, every moment of disconnection, every hint of disapproval as a threat to my survival. No wonder I was exhausted all the time.

Reflection: What's one memory or moment you now see through a different lens?

Shame Versus Truth

What I want you to understand: **Shame isn't truth. It's a story we were handed.**

And we get to rewrite it.

Before I understood RSD, I thought there was something fundamentally wrong with how I processed social interactions. I thought I was weak for caring so much about what others thought. I thought I was broken for having such intense emotional reactions to things that seemed small to everyone else.

But shame had taught me to see intensity as weakness, when intensity is actually one of the gifts of the ADHD brain. We feel things deeply. We care passionately. We notice subtleties in emotion and interaction that others miss.

The problem wasn't the intensity. The problem was that no one had taught me how to work with it.

The Should've Spiral

Let's talk about something real that happens after diagnosis. I call it the "should've spiral."

It goes something like this: "I didn't know why I was struggling. So I assumed it was my fault. So I beat myself up about it. So I started hiding the struggle. And then I felt even more broken."

Then you get diagnosed and suddenly you're thinking: "I should've figured this out sooner. I should've gotten help earlier. I should've been kinder to myself. I should've, I should've, I should've."

That's not healing. That's just shame with a new target.

Here's what I wish someone had told me: **You couldn't see it then, because no one gave you the language to understand it.**

I spent forty years thinking I was just someone who needed "more structure" or was "easily overwhelmed" or "too emotional." These weren't accurate descriptions, they were the closest approximations I could make without the right framework.

You weren't failing. You were adapting without a map.

The Identity Grief

Something else nobody talks about: getting diagnosed can feel like relief and grief at the same time.

Relief because you finally have an answer. Grief because you start to see your whole past through this new lens.

"All those years I thought I was just disorganized, I was actually undiagnosed."

"All those times I thought I was being dramatic, I was actually having a regulation breakdown."

"All those moments I thought I was lazy, I was actually exhausted from working twice as hard as everyone else."

This is what I call identity grief. It's mourning the version of yourself that never got the support they needed. It's feeling sad for the kid who was trying so hard and getting criticized instead of helped.

That grief is valid. And you don't have to rush through it.

When I think about my teenage years, the times I'd shut down completely when overwhelmed, the social situations where I'd say the wrong thing and replay it for weeks, the way I'd get so focused on projects that I'd forget to eat or sleep, I feel a deep sadness for that kid who thought he was just weird.

But I also feel appreciation. Because that kid developed incredible resilience. He learned to read rooms and adapt to diffcrent expectations. He built systems and workarounds that served him for decades. He survived.

Reflection: Write a short message to your younger self who didn't know about ADHD yet. What would you want them to know?

You Weren't Failing, You Were Adapting

The reframe that changed everything for me: **You weren't failing. You were adapting.**

Let me be really specific about what I mean.

When you didn't know why certain things were hard, you made up stories to explain it. Stories like:

- "I'm just not disciplined enough"
- "I'm too sensitive"
- "I can't handle normal adult responsibilities"
- "I'm fundamentally flawed"

But those stories weren't true. They were the best explanations you had with the information available to you.

You were adapting. Surviving. Finding ways to cope with challenges you couldn't name.

And when you couldn't cope? When you melted down or shut down or made mistakes? You weren't failing. You were having a predictable response to an overwhelming situation.

The Reframes That Heal

I want to give you some specific reframes that helped me and might help you:

Old story: "I'm always late because I'm disrespectful."
New story: "I struggle with time perception and transition planning, and I'm learning tools to help with that."

Old story: "I can't stick to anything because I'm flaky."
New story: "I need variety and novelty to maintain engagement, and I'm building systems that work with that."

Old story: "I'm too emotional and dramatic."
New story: "I experience emotions intensely, which is both a challenge and a strength."

Old story: "I can't handle normal adult life."
New story: "I'm managing invisible cognitive load that other people don't have to deal with."

Old story: "I'm just making excuses."
New story: "I'm finally understanding my brain well enough to advocate for what I need."

Notice how the new stories aren't about being perfect or having no challenges. They're about being accurate instead of harsh.

Reflection: Complete this reframe:

- **Old story about yourself:**

- **New, compassionate story:**

The Social Media Wake-Up Call

About a year into my ADHD advocacy journey on social media, I had an experience that really drove home how deeply shame runs in our community.

I posted something and got a comment that absolutely ripped into me. Someone telling me to stop posting about ADHD, that I wasn't special, that I was just making excuses. The usual stuff.

What was interesting was that when I looked at this person's profile, they were in several ADHD support groups. So they weren't anti-ADHD. They were just having a bad day and my post happened to be in their feed.

But what fascinated me: I could feel myself starting to spiral. I was ready to delete all my social media accounts. I was thinking, "I'm wasting everybody's time. I'm embarrassing myself and my family. What was I thinking doing this?"

And then something amazing happened. I stepped outside myself and observed what was happening. I watched my rejection sensitivity in real time.

I still had the emotions. I still felt that familiar sting. But because I understood what was going on, I was able to come out of it much faster.

I actually took a screenshot of the comment, deleted it from my post, blocked the person, and made an entire post about rejection sensitivity using this as a real-time example. It became one of my highest-performing posts.

I wish I could remember that person's name so I could thank them for the inspiration.

That experience taught me something crucial: understanding the mechanism doesn't eliminate the feeling, but it changes your relationship with it. I still felt that familiar sting of rejection. But instead of spiraling into "What's wrong with me?" I could think, "Oh, that's my RSD. This feeling is temporary and not actually about my worth as a person."

This is what reframing shame looks like in practice. It's not about never feeling bad about yourself again. It's about catching those moments and choosing a different response. It's about moving from "I'm broken" to "My brain processes this differently, and that's information, not condemnation."

The Self-Compassion Shift

The opposite of shame isn't pride. It's self-compassion.

Self-compassion isn't about excuses or lowering standards. It's about treating yourself with the same kindness you'd show a good friend who was struggling.

When you make a mistake, instead of "I'm such an idiot," try "That was hard, and I'm still learning."

When you struggle with something, instead of "I should be able to handle this," try "This is genuinely challenging for my brain, and it's okay to need support."

When you feel overwhelmed, instead of "I'm being dramatic," try "I'm feeling a lot right now, and that's information about what I need."

This isn't about positive thinking. It's about accurate thinking. It's about responding to your struggles with curiosity instead of criticism.

The Inherited Shame Stops Here

One of the most powerful motivations for my own healing work has been watching my kids. I don't want them to inherit the shame I carried for so long.

When my son makes a mistake now, instead of him spiraling into "I always mess up," we talk about what happened and what we can learn from it. When my daughter gets overwhelmed, instead of pushing through, we talk about what she needs to feel regulated.

The shame stories that were passed down to me? They stop with me.

And they can stop with you too.

You Deserve Understanding

What I want you to hear: **You deserve understanding. Including your own.**

You don't have to earn compassion by being perfect. You don't have to prove you're worthy of kindness by never struggling.

You're human. You have a brain that works differently. You've been doing the best you can with what you had available.

That's not an excuse. That's a fact.

Reflection: What's something you're ready to forgive yourself for?

The Healing Isn't Linear

I want to be honest with you: this reframing work isn't a one-time thing. Shame has deep roots, and healing happens in layers.

Some days you'll feel compassionate toward yourself. Other days the old voices will be loud. That's normal. That's not failure.

Healing isn't about never feeling shame again. It's about recognizing it when it shows up and choosing a different response.

It's about catching yourself mid-spiral and saying, "Hey, that voice doesn't get to drive anymore."

It's about remembering that you're not broken, you're different. And different isn't wrong.

Moving Forward

Reframing shame isn't about erasing your past or pretending everything was fine. It's about seeing your past with accuracy instead of cruelty.

It's about understanding that you've always been doing the best you could with the tools you had. And now you have better tools.

It's about recognizing that your struggles were real and valid, even if they didn't have a name yet.

It's about choosing compassion over criticism, understanding over judgment, and curiosity over shame.

You're not broken. You never were. You're just finally getting the user manual for your brain.

And that manual starts with one simple truth: you deserve kindness, especially from yourself.

Sidenote: If you're dealing with multiple diagnoses or suspect you might be, the shame can feel even more complex. "What's wrong with me?" becomes "What else is wrong with me?" But the same principle applies: you're not broken, you're getting a clearer picture of how your brain works. Each piece of understanding is a gift, not a burden.

Key takeaways: Shame isn't truth. It's a story you were handed. Every time you choose self-compassion over self-criticism, you're rewriting that story. The healing isn't linear, and that's okay. Progress is choosing curiosity over judgment, understanding over blame.

Chapter 6: The Identity Shift

Who you are when you stop trying to be "normal"

When I got diagnosed, it felt like someone finally handed me the instruction manual to my brain... but all the pages were in code.

I didn't suddenly feel clear or confident. I felt like I'd been handed a whole new version of myself, one I didn't fully recognize yet.

And don't get me wrong, there was relief. I finally had an answer. A name. Something that explained the struggle.

But that relief was tangled up in a kind of quiet grief. Because when the pieces started falling into place, I realized how many years I'd spent blaming myself for things I never understood.

And honestly? That stings.

I started to question everything. "Who was I really?" "Was I just a product of coping mechanisms?" "What parts of me were the real me and what parts were just survival mode?"

That kind of identity shift doesn't happen in a day. It happens slowly, like peeling back layers you didn't know you were wearing.

The Mask You Didn't Know You Were Wearing

Let's go deeper into something I've touched on before: masking. Because once you understand it, you can't unsee how much energy you've been spending on it.

For years, I was chasing this version of "normal." Trying to be the dependable one. The calm one. The one who didn't forget stuff, didn't get overwhelmed by noise, didn't need to pace while thinking.

Basically, I was trying to be the kind of person I thought the world wanted from me.

And I wasn't faking it. I was masking.

Masking isn't about being deceptive. It's about safety. It's when you copy what seems right, how people talk, how they organize, how they show up, not because it's natural, but because it feels safer than being misunderstood.

You watch. You mimic. You adapt. And the more you do it, the more you forget what feels like you and what just feels safe.

I come from a very calm family. We don't react strongly to things. We respond to stressful situations with level heads and measured words. It's actually a good trait to have, and I'm grateful for it.

But what I didn't realize is how much anxiety was going on underneath that calm exterior.

My dad worked a high-stress job for decades, always appearing cool and collected. When he retired, we found out he had a stomach ulcer. All that stress had to go somewhere.

I inherited that same pattern. Calm on the outside, radio stations blaring on the inside.

I didn't have language for any of this until I saw it in someone else. One of my kids, trying so hard to act "normal" in a room full of people, shrinking their quirks, trying not to stim, trying not to interrupt when they had something big to say.

And it hit me like a freight train: "They're doing what I've done my whole life."

And once you see it in them, the way the world tries to shape them into something smaller, you start realizing how early that shaping started in you.

Reflection: How has your sense of identity shifted since learning about your ADHD?

The Confusion After Diagnosis

Getting diagnosed doesn't flip a switch. It opens a door. And half the time, you're not even sure what room you've walked into.

There's this internal journey that kicks off the moment you realize, "Oh. This thing has a name." But the emotional part? That comes in stages.

First, there's **pre-diagnosis**, where you're confused, frustrated, or just constantly wondering why things feel harder than they should. You start believing those negative stories because nothing else makes sense.

Then, there's **diagnosis**, and that's where relief crashes right into disorientation. You finally have a frame, but now you've got to re-hang everything in your brain.

And then comes **post-diagnosis**, and that's the real work. That's where you start rebuilding your self-image. Not just based on who you've been told you are, but who you actually are when you stop trying to pass for "normal."

That's why I say: Diagnosis is just the key. You still have to figure out which doors to unlock.

The Unmasking Process

About a year after my diagnosis, I started what I've heard people call "unmasking", pulling back the layers of adaptation and finding out what was really me underneath.

This was harder than I expected, especially on my marriage.

I had to apologize to my wife multiple times during this process because I was discovering things that had been stressing me out for years, but I'd just learned to make them seem normal.

The person she'd married over 20 years ago would put up with certain things, was more social, would do the things he knew he was supposed to do. Suddenly, I was saying, "Actually, no, I'm not going to that event because I know it's going to overstimulate me," or "I need to change how we handle family dinner because the noise level is overwhelming."

I know that was really hard for her. She married one person, and suddenly that person was different. Not because I was faking before, but because I was finally distinguishing between what I could tolerate and what actually worked for me.

She's incredibly loving and supportive and wants to understand, but that was still a hurdle. Because you expect adolescents to change and figure themselves out, but not your 40-something husband.

The Dinner Table Revolution

Let me give you a concrete example of what unmasking looked like in practice.

We have five kids, and we homeschool, so our house is lively. Dinner time especially could get pretty chaotic. The kids would get excited about their day, stories would overlap, voices would get louder and louder as they tried to be heard over each other.

For years, I'd sit through these dinners getting increasingly overwhelmed, until I'd eventually just get up and leave the room. I'd take my plate and go eat somewhere quiet. I wasn't huffing out or making a scene, I'd just disappear.

I told myself I was being considerate by not telling everyone to quiet down. But what was really happening was that the noise level was hitting my overstimulation threshold, and my brain's solution was to flee.

The problem was that my leaving would kill the vibe. The kids could tell Dad had reached his limit, even if I wasn't saying anything. The happy family moment would just deflate.

After my diagnosis, I learned about sensory processing and overstimulation. I bought some loop earplugs and had a conversation with the family.

"You're going to see me put earplugs in sometimes during dinner," I told them. "This isn't because I don't want to hear you or because you're too loud. These earplugs let me hear you perfectly fine, they just bring the decibels down so I can stay present instead of needing to leave the room."

Game changer.

Now I can stay at the table, be part of the conversation, and not get overwhelmed. The kids don't have to worry about being "too much" for Dad. Everyone gets to be themselves.

This is what unmasking looks like in practice: finding ways to honor your actual needs instead of just enduring what you think you should be able to handle. It's not about demanding the world change for you. It's about making small adjustments that let you show up more authentically.

If you're ready to start your own unmasking process, begin by noticing when you feel most and least like yourself. What environments, people, or activities bring out your authentic self? What situations make you feel like you're performing? That awareness is your starting point.

Reflection: Who are you when you're not trying to pass as "normal"?

The Question You've Never Asked

A question that might feel weird but is incredibly important: **Who are you when you're not trying to pass?**

Who are you when you're not managing how you come across? When you're not editing your energy level, your curiosity, your way of processing information?

For me, the answer was surprising:

I'm someone who interrupts because I'm excited, not because I'm rude. I need space after social events, not because I'm antisocial, but because I'm overstimulated. I think best while pacing in circles, because stillness sometimes jams up my thoughts. I get intensely focused on projects that interest me, sometimes to the exclusion of everything else.

That's me. And getting to say it out loud, without apology, was wild.

I remember one of my coworkers commenting on how I'd pace during phone calls. "Do you know you do that?" they asked.

Old me would have felt embarrassed and tried to sit still. New me said, "Yeah, it helps me think. Movement gets my brain going."

"Huh," they said. "That's actually pretty cool."

That's the difference between masking and authenticity. Instead of hiding the quirk, I owned it. And instead of judgment, I got curiosity.

The Identity Integration Process

This isn't about becoming someone new. It's about becoming who you've always been, but with context.

Think of it like this: You've been living in a house your whole life, but you didn't know there was a basement. The basement was always there. It's part of the house. But now that you know about it, you can understand why the upstairs floors creak the way they do.

The basement is your ADHD. It's been there all along, influencing everything above it. But now you have access to it. You can see how it's been supporting and shaping your whole structure.

Who You Are vs. Who You've Been

There's a difference between who you are and who you've been performing as.

Who you've been performing as might be:

- The person who never asks for help
- The person who says yes to everything

- The person who hides their struggles
- The person who apologizes for taking up space
- The person who tries to be "low maintenance"

Who you actually are might be:

- Someone who thinks out loud and processes verbally
- Someone who has intense focus when interested and struggles when bored
- Someone who feels emotions deeply and needs time to process them
- Someone who notices details others miss
- Someone who has bursts of creativity and periods of rest
- Someone who connects ideas in unexpected ways

Neither version is wrong. But only one of them is sustainable.

Reflection: What's one part of yourself you've been hiding that you're now ready to own?

The Permission to Be Yourself

One of the most powerful shifts in identity work is moving from "I have to hide this" to "I get to be this."

Instead of hiding your need for movement, you get to build walking meetings into your schedule.

Instead of apologizing for your processing style, you get to say, "I think better out loud, give me a second."

Instead of forcing yourself into neurotypical productivity systems, you get to build systems that actually work for your brain.

This isn't about being "difficult" or "high maintenance." It's about being human. About working with your actual operating system instead of against it.

The People Who Get It

Something that happens during identity integration: you start to notice who really sees you and who's been seeing the performance.

Some people will be relieved. They'll say, "This makes so much sense. I always wondered why you seemed stressed about things that looked easy."

Others might be confused or even resistant. They might say, "But you've always been so organized," or "You don't seem like you have ADHD."

That's information. Not about you, but about them. About their understanding of ADHD. About their comfort with authenticity.

You don't need everyone to understand. You just need to stop apologizing for being real.

The Strengths You Didn't Know Were Strengths

Something interesting that happens when you stop trying to be neurotypical: you start to notice the strengths that were always there.

Hyperfocus becomes a strength when you can direct it intentionally.

Emotional intensity becomes empathy and passion when you learn to channel it.

Curiosity becomes innovation when you stop apologizing for your questions.

Pattern recognition becomes strategic thinking when you trust your insights.

Adaptability becomes resilience when you stop seeing it as inconsistency.

These weren't things you developed after diagnosis. They were always part of you. You just couldn't see them clearly through the fog of trying to be someone else.

The Ripple Effect

One of the most beautiful parts of this whole journey: when you start to understand and accept yourself, it ripples out to everyone around you.

My kids have started helping their friends with the ADHD concepts they've learned from watching my content. My 16-year-old daughter told me she went back and watched my videos about body doubling so she could help a friend who was struggling with homework.

"Dad, I'm your biggest fan," she said when I asked how she thought to do that.

I may have cried a little.

But it wasn't just the sweet moment (though that was pretty great). It was seeing how authenticity gives other people permission to be real too.

The Internal Shift

The real identity shift happens internally. It's when you stop monitoring yourself constantly. When you stop asking, "Am I being too much?" and start asking, "What do I need to do my best work?"

It's when you stop apologizing for your brain and start advocating for it.

It's when you stop seeing your ADHD as something to manage and start seeing it as something to understand and work with.

What Changes

When you start to integrate your ADHD identity, several things shift:

Your relationship with your struggles changes. Instead of being ashamed of them, you start to see them as information about what you need.

Your expectations of yourself change. You stop trying to be a neurotypical person with ADHD and start being an ADHD person with your own strengths and challenges.

Your advocacy changes. You stop asking for exceptions and start asking for what works. You become clearer about your needs because you understand them better.

Your relationships change. Some get deeper because you're more authentic. Others might become more distant because you're no longer performing. Both are okay.

The Person You're Becoming

You're not becoming a new person. You're becoming a more conscious version of yourself.

You're someone who:

- Understands their brain well enough to work with it
- Advocates for their needs without apologizing
- Sees ADHD as part of their identity, not a problem to fix
- Builds systems that support their actual operating system
- Chooses authenticity over performance
- Knows the difference between accommodation and hiding

This person was always there. They were just buried under layers of trying to be someone else.

Reflection: How do you want to show up as your authentic self?

The Relief of Being Real

There's a particular kind of relief that comes with stopping the performance. It's the relief of not having to remember how you're supposed to be. Of not having to monitor every word, every reaction, every quirk.

It's the relief of being able to say, "I need a minute to process this" instead of pretending you understood the first time.

It's the relief of being able to move when you need to move, think out loud when you need to think out loud, and take breaks when you need to take breaks.

It's the relief of being human instead of trying to be perfect.

Moving Forward

Identity integration doesn't mean you have to tell everyone about your ADHD or never adapt to social situations. It means you get to choose how much of yourself to share and when.

It means you know who you are clearly enough to make conscious choices about how you show up in different spaces.

It means you stop apologizing for being wired differently and start designing a life that works with your actual brain.

You're not starting over. You're just finally getting to be who you've always been, but with context, compassion, and choice.

And that person? That person is pretty amazing.

Key takeaways: You're not becoming someone new. You're becoming who you've always been, but with context and choice. Unmasking isn't about being difficult; it's about being authentic. When you stop performing "normal" and start living as yourself, it gives everyone around you permission to be real too.

Chapter 7: Systems That Don't Suck (For Your Brain)

You don't need a perfect system. You need a forgiving one.

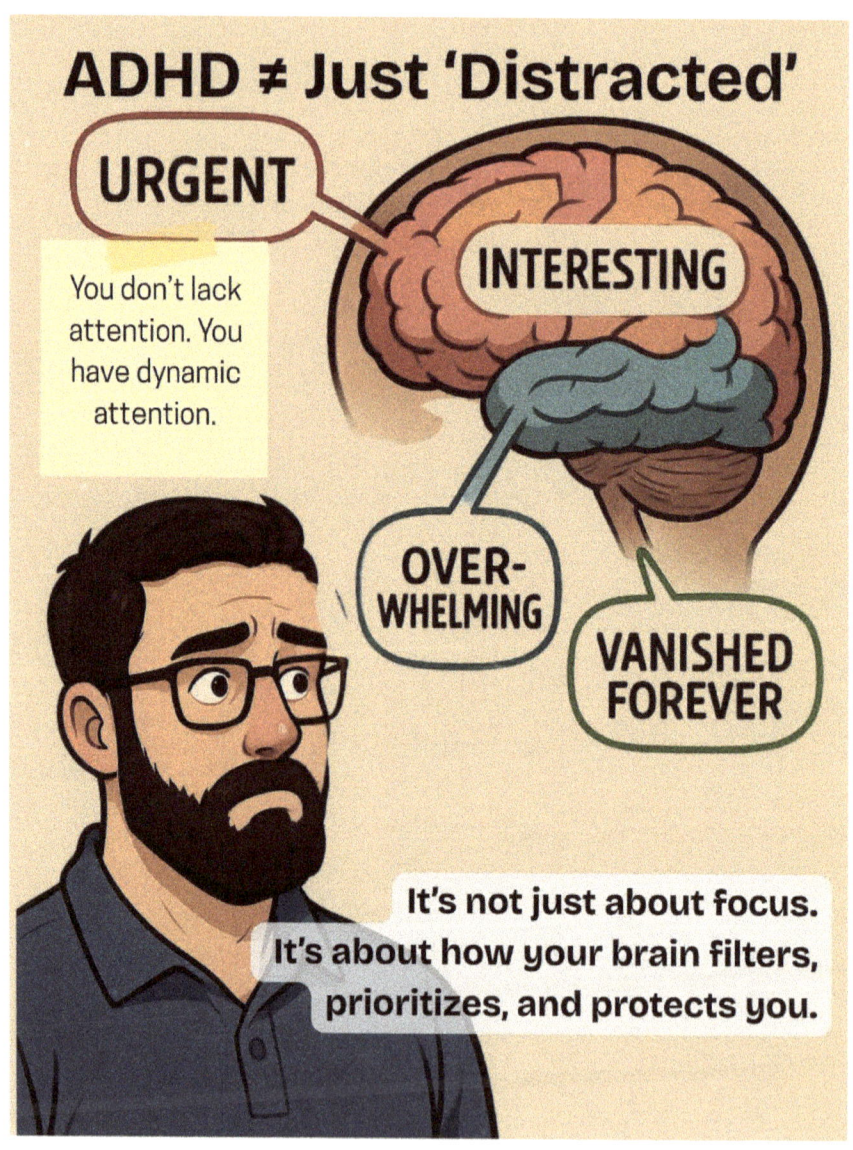

Once you start understanding who you actually are underneath all that masking, the next question becomes: how do you build a life that supports that authentic self?

If one more productivity guru tells me the secret is waking up at 5am and color-coding my calendar, I might spontaneously combust. Because here's the truth no one tells you: **You're not struggling because you lack effort. You're struggling because the systems were never designed for your brain.**

So let's drop the guilt. This chapter isn't about doing things the "right" way. It's about finding what actually helps, especially on the days when motivation is nowhere to be found and you've already lost your keys twice before 10am.

We're building a toolkit. Not a rulebook. And the best toolkits? They evolve. They shift based on your energy, your environment, your season of life.

Which means if something stopped working? That's not failure. That's feedback.

The Myth of the Perfect System

Let me tell you about my system graveyard.

I've tried the color-coded bullet journal (abandoned after three weeks when I couldn't find the right colored pens). I've built elaborate Notion dashboards with 14 different views (used exactly twice). I've downloaded apps with dopamine-triggering sounds and little productivity trees (deleted when the notifications became overwhelming).

And for maybe a week, each one felt like I'd cracked the code. I'd think, "This is it! This is how I finally become a functioning adult!"

But then life happens. Or hormones. Or a stressful week. Or just Tuesday.

And the whole thing unravels. So I'd blame myself.

"I'm just not disciplined enough." "I need to try harder." "Everyone else seems to make this work."

But no one told us: **The system wasn't built for your brain. It was built for consistency over adaptability. For predictability over pattern. For control over curiosity.**

So it worked until you needed grace.

Living Systems vs. Static Systems

What I learned from homeschooling five kids while working from home: rigid systems break the moment real life shows up.

Our first attempt at a homeschool schedule looked like something from a magazine. Color-coded subjects, perfectly timed blocks, educational activities planned down to the minute.

It lasted exactly three days.

Why? Because my son learns better while pacing. My daughter needs music to focus. One kid is a morning person, another doesn't want to wake up until 10am. One thrives on structure, another rebels against it.

The perfect schedule couldn't accommodate the actual humans using it.

So we built what I call a "living system" instead. Anchor points, not rigid schedules. Rhythms, not rules.

We still get everything done. But the system bends to fit our actual brains instead of demanding our brains conform to some theoretical ideal.

Reflection: What kind of system (even a simple one) helps you return to center when things fall apart?

We Don't Need Perfection. We Need Forgiveness.

Let's flip the script. Routines aren't the enemy. But rigid routines? The ones that expect you to show up the same way every day? They collapse the second ADHD enters the chat.

Because ADHD isn't linear. It's rhythmic. Pattern-based. Intermittent. Adaptive.

Many of us don't run on checklists. We run on context.

And when a system doesn't flex? It doesn't just fail. It shames us in the process.

The perfect productivity system says: "Do A, then B, then C, at exactly these times, in exactly this way."

A forgiving system says: "These three things matter today. There are several ways to approach them. When it all goes sideways, start here."

Your system didn't fail because you're unreliable. It failed because it didn't flex.

That's why I'm not here to hand you another perfect routine. You don't need one. You need scaffolding. You need systems that forgive.

Ones that help you return, not ones that punish you for drifting.

Anchors, Not Agendas

So let's talk about anchors. Not the kind that drag you down. The kind that hold you steady.

Most planners assume you run on appointments. But many ADHD brains? We run on patterns. Rhythms. Context cues. Dopamine windows.

That's why strict scheduling, with perfectly timed 30-minute blocks, often backfires. You miss one thing and the whole grid collapses.

Instead, think about **anchor points.** Natural reset moments that already exist in your day:

- Waking up (however that happens)
- Breakfast
- Lunch break (even if it's eating crackers at your desk)
- End of work (official or unofficial)
- Bedtime routine (however loose)

You don't have to force your brain into a rigid flow. You can **wrap routines around what's already there.**

In our house, we have morning anchor points that work with everyone's natural rhythms:

- When you wake up (not a specific time), drink water and eat
- After breakfast, check the plan for the day
- Mid-morning, we do focused work while energy is good
- After lunch, we do more collaborative or creative tasks
- Late afternoon is for life stuff (chores, errands, free time)

No rigid schedule. No guilt if someone sleeps in or needs a different rhythm on a particular day. But enough structure that everyone knows what to expect.

Anchors don't require discipline. They just ask you to notice what's already happening.

Reflection: What are your natural anchor points throughout the day?

The One-Box System

When your brain is busy, make it easy to focus on what actually matters.

Most productivity systems want you to categorize everything. Sort by priority, urgency, project, context. But that's a lot of cognitive load for a brain that's already maxed out.

Instead, try the **One-Box System:**

What matters most? (The thing that, if you did nothing else, would make today feel worthwhile)

What needs done? (The stuff that has to happen, even if it's boring)

What I'll forgive? (The stuff that can wait, and you won't beat yourself up about it)

That's it. Three categories. One mental framework.

Let me show you how this worked during one of my most chaotic periods, when we were getting my son assessed while I was dealing with a major work deadline:

- **Matters most:** Be present for my son's evaluation appointment (everything else could wait if needed)
- **Needs done:** Finish client presentation, pick up groceries for dinner
- **Will forgive:** Organizing the garage, responding to non-urgent emails, that LinkedIn article I'd been meaning to write

On a different day, when I was in a better headspace, my One-Box looked completely different:

- **Matters most:** Have an uninterrupted conversation with my wife about our homeschool plans
- **Needs done:** Three client calls, laundry, kids' math lessons
- **Will forgive:** Updating my website, cleaning out my email, researching that new productivity app

The beauty of this system is it flexes with your actual capacity, not your theoretical capacity.

Forgiveness isn't a weakness. It's the reason you'll come back to the system tomorrow.

Scaffolds, Not Schedules

Let's talk about what actually works for many ADHD brains. Because despite what all those "optimize your life" blogs say, you don't need an elite morning routine to be productive. You need scaffolding.

Scaffolding isn't about micromanaging your day. It's about building light support structures that help you get started, stay focused, and come back when you drift.

What scaffolding looks like in my actual life:

- A **visual timer** on my desk that gives me gentle awareness of time passing
- A **sticky note** on my monitor that says "Breathe. Then start with one small thing."
- A **consistent workspace** set up the same way each day so my brain doesn't have to make setup decisions
- A **closing routine** where I write tomorrow's "matters most" before I shut down
- A **text thread** with my brother where we check in about our daily priorities

If it helps you show up? It counts.

You're not undisciplined. You're scaffold-dependent. And that's okay.

Reflection: If you could focus on three things today, what would they be?

- What matters most:
- What needs done:
- What you'll forgive:

The Family Scaffold Example

Let me give you a concrete example of how scaffolding works in practice.

With five kids, our evening routine used to be chaos. Kids wouldn't know what was expected, I'd get overwhelmed by all the tasks, someone would have a meltdown, and bedtime would stretch on forever.

So we built scaffolding:

Visual checklist posted where everyone can see it (brush teeth, put on pajamas, pick out tomorrow's clothes, one story)

Music playlist that's exactly 45 minutes long (when the music stops, it's time for lights out)

Rotation system for who gets extra snuggle time (removes the negotiation)

Buffer time built in for the inevitable "I need water" or "I can't find my stuffed animal"

The routine isn't rigid. Some nights we skip story time if someone's tired. Some nights we add extra snuggle time if someone needs it. But the scaffolding gives us a framework to return to.

When Systems Break Down

Let's be real: systems break down. Not because you're doing it wrong, but because life is unpredictable and ADHD brains need variety.

When your system stops working, instead of throwing it all away and starting over, ask:

- What part of this was actually helping?
- What part was creating friction?
- What's different about my life that this system needs to evolve?

Maybe you need more flexibility. Maybe you need more structure. Maybe you need more recovery time built in.

I went through a phase where I was obsessed with time-blocking every minute of my day. It worked great for about two weeks. Then I started feeling suffocated by my own schedule.

Instead of abandoning the concept entirely, I kept what worked (blocking time for deep work) and dropped what didn't (scheduling every email check and bathroom break).

Systems that last aren't the ones that run perfectly. They're the ones you return to, even after they've been broken.

The Forgiving System Principles

The principles that make systems work for many ADHD brains:

Start where you are, not where you think you should be. If you can only handle one anchor point, start there. You can always add more later.

Build in flexibility. Your system should bend, not break, when life gets messy. Plan for the fact that some days will be different.

Make it easier to return than to start. The goal isn't never falling off. It's getting back on quickly without shame.

Celebrate small wins. Did you remember to drink water? That counts. Did you write one sentence? That counts too.

Design for your worst day, not your best. When you're tired, stressed, or overwhelmed, what's the absolute minimum that would still feel helpful?

The Context-Switching Problem

One thing traditional productivity systems don't account for: many people with ADHD struggle with context switching.

Going from deep work to answering emails to attending a meeting to making lunch isn't just a schedule change. It's a complete cognitive reorganization each time.

So instead of fighting context switches, I minimize them:

Batching similar tasks (all calls on Tuesday morning, all writing on Wednesday afternoon)

Transition buffers (10 minutes between meetings to decompress and refocus)

Context cues (different music for different types of work, different locations when possible)

Energy matching (creative work when energy is high, administrative work when it's lower)

This isn't about being precious or high-maintenance. It's about working with how your brain actually operates instead of forcing it into someone else's workflow.

Reflection: What's one forgiving principle you want to build into your systems?

What Actually Matters

At the end of the day, the best system is the one you'll actually use. Not the one that looks impressive in a screenshot, but the one that works with your brain on a Tuesday when you're tired and distracted.

Start simple. Build your own frameworks. Add complexity only when the simple version stops working.

I've tried dozens of productivity systems over the years. The one that's stuck is embarrassingly simple:

- Start each day by asking: "What's the one thing that matters most today?"
- End each day by asking: "What's the one thing that matters most tomorrow?"
- When I get overwhelmed, return to those two questions

That's it. No color coding. No complex workflows. No apps with seventeen features.

Just two questions that help me focus on what actually matters instead of getting lost in the productivity theater.

You don't need to change who you are. You just need to give your brain the support it's been asking for.

The System That Sticks

I want to leave you with this: **The system that sticks isn't the one that controls your life. It's the one that supports your life.**

It's not about forcing yourself into someone else's mold. It's about understanding your brain well enough to build something that actually fits.

Your system might look different every season. It might need tweaking every few months. It might be simpler than you think it should be.

That's not failure. That's adaptation. That's working with your brain instead of against it.

And that? That's the beginning of something sustainable.

Key takeaways: You don't need perfect systems. You need forgiving ones. Build around your natural anchor points, design for your worst days (not your best), and remember: systems that last aren't the ones that run perfectly, they're the ones you return to after they've been broken.

Chapter 8: Tools, Not Rules

You need a toolkit that works with your brain, especially on hard days

You don't need more rules. You need more tools.

And tools aren't permanent. They're not tattoos. They're not life sentences. They're helpers. And helpers change.

You might outgrow a tool. You might forget it exists for a while. You might come back to it later and think, "Oh. That actually helps again."

That's not inconsistency. That's adaptation.

You're not failing for switching tools. You're problem-solving. And that's powerful.

Let me tell you about my magnet fidget. Right now, I've got this little magnetic thing in my hand that I'm swiveling around while I think. I didn't even realize I was doing it until someone on a video call mentioned it.

"Do you know you're constantly playing with something?" they asked.

Old me would have felt embarrassed and tried to sit perfectly still. New me said, "Yeah, it helps me focus. Keeps my hands busy so my brain can concentrate."

That's the difference between rules and tools. Rules would say "sit still and pay attention." Tools say "find what helps you pay attention, then use it."

The Lie We've Been Sold

Let's talk about the lie we've all been sold: "You just need to get motivated."

Nope. **Motivation is a mood.** And ADHD doesn't always RSVP to the mood party.

But **activation**? That's a process. You can build it, like stacking Lego bricks.

Most productivity advice assumes you'll feel like doing the thing. But many people with ADHD need to start before we feel ready. We need tools that help us begin, not tools that wait for us to want to begin.

The Problem With Rules

Rules are rigid. Rules assume you'll show up the same way every day. Rules don't account for hormones, sleep, stress, or the fact that sometimes your brain just isn't cooperating.

Tools are different. Tools adapt. Tools meet you where you are.

Rule: "I will work out every morning at 6am."

Tool: "I have three movement options: 20-minute walk, 10-minute stretch, or dancing to two songs. I pick based on my energy and time."

See the difference? The rule breaks the moment you oversleep. The tool flexes with your reality.

Reflection: What's one tool you tried that actually helped (even if it felt weird or silly at first)?

Your Sensory Stack

Let's start with something most people skip: your sensory needs.

Before you can focus, you need to feel regulated. Before you can think clearly, your nervous system needs to feel safe.

I learned this the hard way when I transitioned from working in a hospital (with constant movement, variety, and clear tasks) to working from home at a desk. Suddenly, I was supposed to sit still and think all day.

My brain rebelled. I'd watch YouTube videos for hours, not because I didn't care about my work, but because my nervous system was seeking the stimulation it was used to.

Your Sensory Stack has three parts:

What calms you:

The tools that help when you're overstimulated

- Loop earplugs (because the world is loud and your brain notices everything)
- Soft lighting (because fluorescents feel aggressive)
- Weighted blankets or lap pads (because pressure is soothing)
- Noise-canceling headphones (because silence is golden)

What alerts you:

The tools that help when you're understimulated

- Cold water on your face (because shock works)
- Peppermint gum or essential oil (because scent is activating)
- Standing or walking (because movement wakes up the brain)
- Bright light or going outside (because your brain thinks it's time to work)

What anchors you:

The tools that help you stay grounded

- Fidget cubes or magnetic toys (because thinking happens in your hands)
- Rocking or swivel chairs (because rhythm is regulating)
- Textures you like (because touch is information)
- Consistent scents or sounds (because familiarity is calming)

This isn't about looking organized. It's about feeling supported.

To build your sensory stack, spend a week paying attention to your environment and responses. Not analyzing or judging, just noticing:

- What environments make you feel immediately calm and focused?
- What helps when you're feeling scattered or overwhelmed?
- When do you feel most grounded and present?
- What sounds, textures, or lighting make you feel more alert?
- What makes you want to escape or shut down?

Keep simple notes: "Felt great during the meeting in the conference room with natural light" or "Couldn't think clearly in the noisy coffee shop." This is data about your nervous system, not personality quirks to apologize for.

Reflection: What does your sensory stack look like?

- What calms you when overstimulated:
- What alerts you when understimulated:
- What anchors you when scattered:

The Body Doubling Discovery

Let me tell you about one of the most powerful tools I've discovered, through a story that changed how I think about ADHD support:

Body doubling is having another person present while you work. They don't have to be working on the same thing, they don't have to be watching you, they just have to be there.

I mentioned earlier the coworker who was constantly missing deadlines but could solve problems that stumped everyone else. What I didn't tell you was how we actually solved his deadline issue, and how it introduced me to one of the most powerful tools I've discovered.

After he mentioned his ADHD diagnosis, I said, "Cool. We're going to change how we do this."

I set up what I called a "working session." "I don't know your work like you do," I told him. "But I have my own stuff to work on. How about you just share your screen and work like you normally would, headphones, music, whatever. I'll be here doing my own thing, but if you need to brainstorm or have questions, I'm available."

He knocked out everything he'd been behind on. Weeks worth of work, done in one session.

That's when I really understood: this wasn't about accountability or supervision. There's something about having another person present that helps ADHD brains focus.

Since then, I've used body doubling countless times. When I'm struggling to start a project, I'll check who's available on Teams at work. "Hey, you got a few minutes to help me out? I just need someone to be on a call while I work through this thing."

Most people are happy to help, especially when they understand it's not complicated. They can do their own work, we might chat occasionally, but mostly it's just shared presence.

The Magic of "Dad, I'm Your Biggest Fan"

One of my proudest moments as a parent happened because of body doubling.

My 16-year-old daughter came to me with this story: Her friend was really struggling with schoolwork, falling behind, getting stressed about it. So my daughter called him up and said, "Hey, how about we just stay on the phone while you do your work?"

She didn't explain what she was doing or why. She just offered to be present while he tackled his assignments.

He got caught up on everything. Weeks worth of work, done in one session.

When she told me about it, I was amazed. "What made you think to do that?" I asked.

"Dad, I'm your biggest fan," she said. "I went back and watched your videos about body doubling and thought it might help."

I may have teared up a little.

But it wasn't just the sweet moment (though that was pretty great). It was seeing how these tools ripple out. She learned something that helped her help a friend. That friend now has a strategy he can use again. The impact keeps spreading.

The Try, Tweak, Toss Philosophy

The uncomfortable truth: most tools will eventually stop working. Not because they're bad tools, but because your brain needs variety.

I've been through phases with different organizational systems, different apps, different routines. What works amazingly for three months might suddenly feel stale or overwhelming.

When a tool stops working, instead of feeling like you failed, ask:

- What part of this was actually helping?
- What part was creating friction?
- What's different about my life that this tool needs to evolve?

Then apply the **Try, Tweak, Toss** philosophy:

Try: Experiment with something new for at least a week

Tweak: Adjust what's almost working instead of abandoning it

Toss: Let go of tools that aren't serving you (without guilt)

Every "failed" tool is actually data about how your brain works.

I keep a note in my phone called "Tools That Worked" where I list things that have been helpful, even if I'm not using them right now.

When I need a reset or my current approach isn't working, I can look back and see what might be worth trying again.

The Activation Stack

Remember how motivation isn't reliable? Here's how to build activation instead:

Layer 1: Cue (Something small and visible that reminds you)

- Sticky note on your laptop that says "Open the document"
- Phone alarm with a gentle message like "Time to start small"
- Calendar block that says "Begin" (not "Finish entire project")

Layer 2: Container (Give your brain a boundary)

- 15-minute timer (not a productivity marathon)
- "Just open the file" (not "finish the project")
- "Write one paragraph" (not "complete the whole report")

Layer 3: Reward (A dopamine bump)

- Music you love playing in the background
- A small piece of chocolate after you start
- Checking something off your list
- Texting someone "I did the thing"

Layer 4: Accountability (A gentle nudge)

- Text someone: "I'm starting this. Ask me later how it went."
- Work while someone else is working (body doubling)
- Share your progress on social media
- Schedule a follow-up conversation about it

You don't have to feel ready. You just need a runway.

Tools for Hard Days

The real test of a tool isn't whether it works on your best days. It's whether it works on your worst days.

Hard day tools need to be:

- Extremely simple (no complex decision-making required)
- Low cognitive load (your brain is already maxed out)
- Immediately comforting (you need support, not challenge)
- Effective when you're tired, stressed, or overwhelmed

Examples of hard day tools:

- Pre-written text to send when you need to cancel: "I'm not feeling great today and need to reschedule. How does [specific alternative time] work for you?"
- Playlist of songs that reliably improve your mood
- List of three things that always help when you're stuck (walk, shower, call friend)
- Permission slip you can read to yourself: "Today I only have to do the essential things, and that's enough"
- Comfort object that fits in your pocket (smooth stone, fidget ring, essential oil)

Reflection: What would be in your "hard day toolkit" (the things that help when everything feels difficult)?

The ADHD-Friendly Tool Showcase

Let's normalize the fact that people with ADHD often benefit from tools that might look unconventional to others:

Time and Task Management:

- Visual timers (because time needs to be visible, not just felt)
- Sticky note systems (because out of sight is out of mind)
- Voice memos to yourself (because sometimes talking is easier than writing)
- Body doubling apps or co-working sessions (because presence helps focus)

Sensory Support:

- Noise-canceling headphones (because the world is loud and very distracting)
- Fidget toys that don't annoy others (because hands need something to do)
- Standing desks or balance balls (because stillness can jam up your thoughts)
- Weighted lap pads (because pressure is calming)

Emotional Regulation:

- Feelings wheel printout (because naming emotions helps process them)
- Breathing apps with gentle reminders (because regulation needs practice)
- Comfort items at your desk (because soothing is productive)
- Affirmation cards (because self-talk needs upgrading)

Organization:

- Clear containers (because you need to see what you have)
- Label makers (because naming things reduces cognitive load)
- Basket systems (because everything needs a home, but it doesn't have to be perfect)
- One-touch rule (because complicated filing systems break down)

If it helps you show up? It counts.

The Co-Worker's Body Doubling Request

I want to share one more body doubling story because it shows how these tools can work for anyone.

A few months ago, one of my co-workers called me out of the blue. "Can we do that thing?" he asked. "That thing where you're with somebody else and it helps you focus?"

"Body doubling?" I asked.

"Yeah, that. I have this deadline and I just cannot push through it. I've been staring at this document for two hours."

We got on a call. He shared his screen. I worked on my own stuff. We barely talked.

Thirty minutes in, he said, "Dude, I'm done. That's everything I needed to finish."

He'd blocked off half a day for this task and finished it in half an hour, just by having someone else present.

This is why I love these tools. They're not just for people with ADHD. They're for anyone whose brain needs a little extra support to do its best work.

Building Your Personal Toolkit

Your toolkit should be as unique as you are. Here's how to build one:

Start with one challenge. Don't try to solve everything at once. Pick one area where you consistently struggle.

Identify what you need. Do you need more activation? More regulation? More organization? More recovery?

Experiment. Try 2-3 different approaches to the same challenge.

Give it time. Most tools need at least a week to show whether they're helpful.

Adjust. Very few tools work perfectly right out of the box.

Build gradually. Add one new tool at a time, not ten.

Reflection: What's one tool you want to try, and what's one you're ready to stop forcing?

The Tool Permission Slip

Before we wrap up, here's your official permission slip:

- You're allowed to use tools that other people don't need
- You're allowed to stop using tools that aren't helping you anymore
- You're allowed to combine tools in ways that work for you
- You're allowed to invest in tools that make your life easier
- You're allowed to keep experimenting until you find what fits

Your brain works differently. Your tools can too.

The Real Goal

The real goal isn't to become a productivity machine. It's to build a life that feels sustainable and authentic.

Tools are just tools. They're not magic. They're not cures. They're not permanent solutions.

But they can be the difference between struggling alone and having support. Between feeling overwhelmed and feeling equipped. Between fighting your brain and working with it.

You deserve to have the tools you need to live the life you want.

And that life? It's not about perfect productivity. It's about showing up as yourself, doing what matters to you, and having the support you need to make it sustainable.

That's what tools are really for.

Key takeaways: Tools adapt to meet you where you are; rules expect you to show up the same way every day. Your toolkit should be as unique as you are. If a tool stops working, that's not failure, that's your brain needing variety. Build your sensory stack, find your activation methods, and remember: if it helps you show up, it counts.

Chapter 9: Talking About It

How to explain ADHD to others (when you choose to)

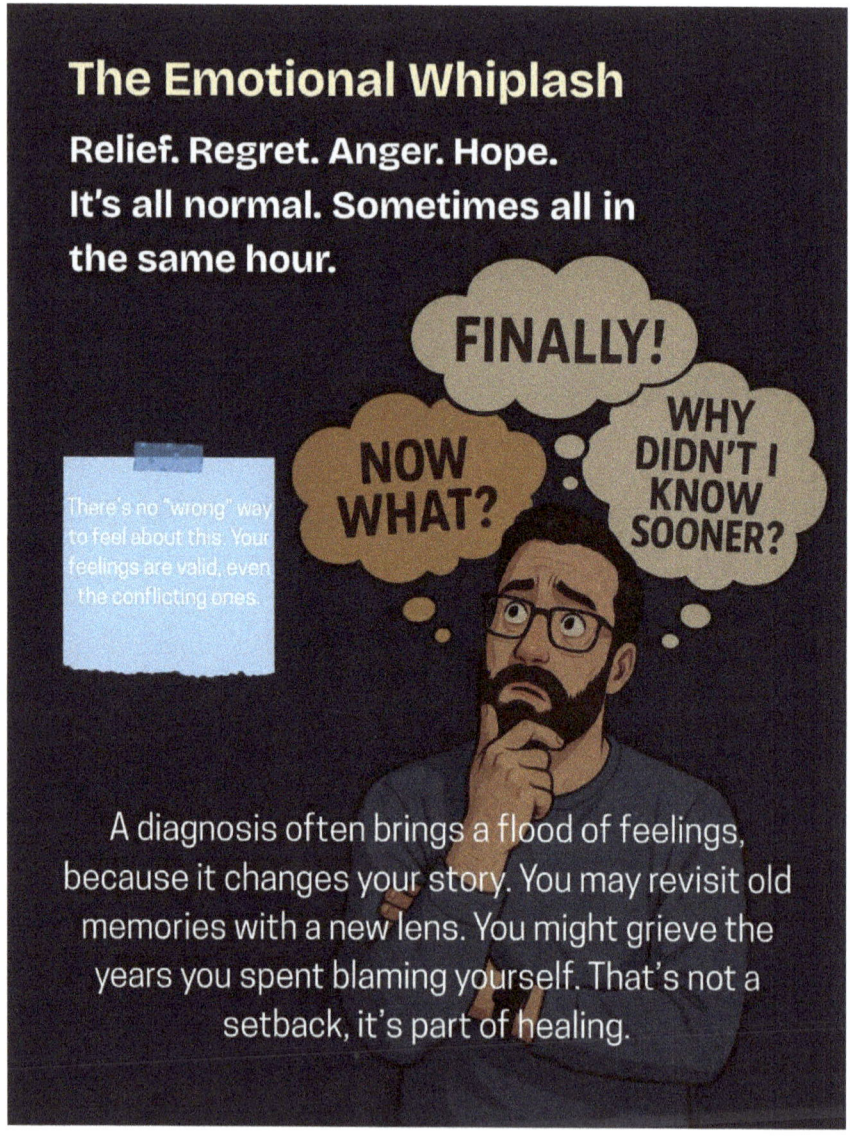

Now that you understand your brain and have tools that help, you might be wondering: who should know about this?

You don't owe anyone your diagnosis. But when you choose to share it, you get to set the tone with clarity, not shame.

Let's start there, because this isn't about getting approval. It's about giving yourself permission. Permission to speak honestly. Permission to ask for support. Permission to stop managing every moment alone.

If you've ever hesitated to speak up, or pulled back from asking for help, I want you to know that's not weakness. That's experience. You've probably been burned before.

But you get to choose who gets a front-row seat to your story. Not everyone earns that seat. And you get to decide when, or if, to offer it.

My Accidental Advocacy Journey

I never planned to become someone who talks openly about ADHD. It happened by accident.

I was trying to build a personal brand on LinkedIn for my strategy consulting work. The posts about IT and business strategy were getting maybe 10 likes and zero comments. I was basically posting into the void.

Then one day, I decided to share a brief post about my ADHD diagnosis. Not because I was trying to make a statement, it was just part of my story.

That post got more engagement than anything I'd ever shared.

Someone from work reached out privately: "I read your LinkedIn post. Please keep writing about that."

It was the first time anyone had asked me to write about anything. So I did a few more posts about ADHD and how it affected my work life.

And something interesting started happening. People began reaching out to me privately. Not commenting publicly, but sending direct messages. Telling me my posts were helping them understand themselves. Saying they'd shared my content with their kids or partners. Some said they'd gone and gotten diagnosed because of what they'd read.

That's when I realized: there were a lot of people who needed to hear this, but weren't getting the information anywhere else.

The Hidden Audience

What I learned about who's actually listening when you talk about ADHD:

Looking at my analytics across platforms, about 75% of my public engagement comes from women. They like posts, leave comments, share content. They're comfortable interacting publicly.

But the people who reach out to me privately? Almost exclusively men. Usually late 30s and up. People who've been reading my content for months without ever interacting with it publicly.

They'll send messages like: "I've been following your posts for six months. This is the first time I've reached out to anyone about this. I think I might have ADHD. I don't know what to do."

Or: "Your post about rejection sensitivity made me cry. I've never told anyone about the thoughts that keep me up at night. Thank you for making me feel less alone."

The stigma is real, especially for men and people who were raised with "just tough it out" and "don't air your problems in public." But when someone does speak honestly about ADHD, it creates permission for others to recognize themselves.

Deciding When to Share

Since disclosure is a choice, let's talk about how to make that choice without spinning out.

Ask yourself these questions:

Who might benefit from understanding your ADHD? (That could be a manager, a teacher, a partner, or even a friend who keeps saying, "You're so smart, why can't you just...?")

What kind of support are you hoping for? (Maybe it's flexibility. Maybe it's space. Maybe it's just not being interrupted when you're mid-sentence.)

Is this person or setting safe? (This one matters more than anything. Because if the answer is "I'm not sure," that's your cue to slow way down.)

This isn't about whether someone deserves to know. It's about whether sharing will help you, not hurt you.

Reflection: What's your personal way of explaining ADHD to someone who matters to you?

Conversation Starters

Some low-pressure, high-integrity conversation starters you can keep in your back pocket:

"I've been learning my brain works a bit differently, especially around focus."
Honest, simple, and opens the door without forcing it.

"This isn't an excuse. It's a heads-up on how I show up best."
You're anchoring the conversation in self-awareness, not apology.

"I'm not looking for advice. I just wanted to share where I'm at."
Huge for dodging the unsolicited "have you tried meditation?" crowd.

"My brain processes things differently sometimes. I might need things repeated or written down."
Practical and specific without being clinical.

"I work better with clear expectations and regular check-ins."
Focuses on what helps rather than what's hard.

These aren't about performing a diagnosis. They're about protecting your capacity while giving people useful information.

When People Don't Get It

Sometimes, even when you share honestly, even when you've practiced the words and shown up with courage, people still won't get it.

And that can hurt. Especially when it's a boss. Or a parent. Or someone you love.

But that pain doesn't mean you did it wrong. It doesn't mean your words failed. And it absolutely doesn't mean you shouldn't have tried.

If someone won't listen, that doesn't make you less credible. It makes them less curious.

It's not your job to drag someone into understanding. Your job is to tell the truth with understanding, not with desperation.

There's a difference between advocacy and emotional labor. You can tell your story without handing it to people who haven't shown they'll carry it with care.

Boundary Phrases

Not every conversation ends with understanding. Some people will want to help but in ways that aren't actually helpful. Others might challenge you, or push back, or offer unsolicited advice.

So let's equip you with some boundary phrases:

"I'm not open to advice, but I appreciate your support."
Kind, clear, no wiggle room.

"I'm still figuring this out. No pressure to 'get it.'"
Takes the tension off the other person while protecting your process.

"You don't have to understand it. I just need space to work with it."
Powerful. And true.

"I'm not asking for a diagnosis debate. This is what's true for me."
 For the people who want to play devil's advocate.

"I appreciate the suggestion, but I'm working with a professional on this."
Redirects well-meaning but unhelpful advice.

Boundaries aren't walls. They're doors with locks, and you hold the key.

Reflection: What's one boundary phrase you want to practice for when conversations go sideways?

The Workplace Conversation

Let's get specific about workplace disclosure, because this is where a lot of people get stuck.

You don't have to disclose to get good work done. But disclosure can sometimes make work easier and more sustainable.

Consider disclosing if:

- You need specific accommodations to do your job well
- Your manager is generally supportive and solution-focused
- You're struggling in ways that might affect your performance
- You work in an environment that has proven values around diversity and inclusion

Consider not disclosing if:

- You're in a toxic work environment
- Your manager has shown bias against people with disabilities
- You're worried about career advancement consequences
- You haven't established credibility yet

If you do disclose, focus on:

- What you need to do your best work
- How this information helps the team succeed
- Specific solutions, not just problems
- Your strengths and how ADHD contributes to them

Here's how that might sound in practice:

"I wanted to let you know that I have ADHD, which affects how I process information and manage tasks. I've learned that I do my best work when I have clear deadlines, written follow-ups after meetings, and the flexibility to take short breaks when I need to recharge. I'm not asking for special treatment, these are just the conditions where I can contribute most effectively to our team goals."

Notice how this frames ADHD as information that helps you work better together, not as a problem that needs accommodating.

The Family Conversation

Family conversations about ADHD can be some of the hardest, because family members often have the strongest reactions and the longest memories.

They might say things like:

- "But you were fine as a kid"
- "Everyone has trouble focusing sometimes"
- "You don't need medication, you just need discipline"
- "Are you sure you're not just making excuses?"

You can respond with:

- "I'm learning about how my brain works. This helps me make sense of things."
- "I appreciate your concern, but I'm working with professionals on this."
- "This isn't about excuses. It's about understanding."
- "I needed you to know because it affects how I show up in the world."

Remember: You can't control their reaction. You can only control your response.

The Ripple Effect

One of the most beautiful parts of speaking openly about ADHD: watching how the conversation ripples out.

I've had people tell me they shared my content with their kids, their partners, their coworkers. I've heard from parents who finally understood why their child was struggling. I've heard from spouses who said, "This is what I've been trying to tell you about yourself for years."

The ripple effect goes beyond just individual understanding. It's about normalizing the conversation. Making it okay to talk about how our brains work differently.

Every time someone shares their story, it makes it easier for the next person to speak up.

What You Don't Have to Explain

Finally, let's talk about what you don't have to explain or justify:

- Why you need the accommodations you need
- Why you can do some things but not others
- Why medication is or isn't right for you
- Why you were diagnosed "late"
- Why you're "high-functioning" but still struggle
- Why you can't just "try harder"

You don't have to make your ADHD make sense to other people. You just have to make it make sense to you.

Reflection: What's one thing you want people to know about your ADHD, and one thing you don't have to explain?

Moving Forward

The real goal of talking about ADHD isn't to get everyone to understand. It's to build a life where you can show up authentically and get the support you need.

Sometimes that means sharing. Sometimes it means not sharing. Sometimes it means sharing with some people and not others.

You get to choose. And you get to change your mind as you learn and grow.

The most important conversation about ADHD is the one you have with yourself. The one where you decide you're worthy of understanding, support, and kindness.

Everything else builds from there.

Sidenote: If you have multiple diagnoses, disclosure becomes more complex. You might choose to share ADHD but not autism, or talk about anxiety but not ADHD. That's completely valid. You get to control how much or how little you share, and with whom. There's no rule that says you have to disclose everything or nothing.

Key takeaways: Sharing your diagnosis is a choice, not an obligation. When you do choose to share, you get to set the tone. You don't have to make your ADHD make sense to other people. You just have to make it make sense to you. Boundaries aren't walls; they're doors with locks, and you hold the key.

Chapter 10: Moving Forward

You're not starting over. You're starting with the right map.

Here we are. The final chapter.

And before we go any further, I want to offer a moment of breath. Because if you've made it this far, it means something clicked. Not everything. Not perfectly. But something in you said, "This is worth exploring."

That matters. You matter.

If you're sitting with thoughts like "I feel like I wasted so many years" or "Everyone else seems so far ahead" or "I finally understand myself, now what?" let me offer this:

You're not starting over. You're starting with context.

All those years you thought you were struggling? You were actually adapting without a manual. Building systems, developing resilience, learning to navigate a world that wasn't designed for how your brain works.

You weren't behind. You were surviving. And now? Now you have language for what you've always known about yourself.

What Progress Actually Looks Like

After everything we've explored, here's what I want you to understand about progress:

It's not about speed. Better to show up imperfectly than to wait for the perfect moment that never comes.

It's not about comparison. Your journey doesn't have to look like anyone else's to be valid.

It's not about elimination. You don't have to stop having ADHD challenges to be making progress.

It's about understanding. The more you know about how your brain works, the more you can work with it instead of against it.

It's about choice. Every time you choose compassion over criticism, you're making progress. Every time you choose a system that fits instead of forcing yourself into one that doesn't, you're making progress.

It's about integration. You're not trying to become someone else. You're trying to become a more conscious, supported version of yourself.

Progress doesn't look like a straight line. It looks like loops, pauses, circles, backtracks, tiny pivots, big resets. And sometimes? It looks like rest.

Reflection: Where do you already see signs of progress (even if small)?

Your Personal Roadmap

You don't need a five-year plan. You need a map for right now.

Your anchors: What grounds you when everything feels chaotic?

- People who see and accept you
- Routines that feel supportive, not rigid
- Places where you feel calm and focused
- Activities that restore your energy

Your boundaries: What protects your wellbeing?

- Saying no to things that drain you
- Asking for what you need without apologizing
- Taking breaks before you burn out
- Choosing authenticity over performance

Your tools: What actually supports you?

- Systems that work with your brain, not against it
- Sensory supports that help you regulate
- People who understand and encourage you
- Resources you can turn to when things get hard

Your values: What matters most to you?

- Connection over achievement
- Progress over perfection
- Sustainability over speed
- Authenticity over approval

This map isn't permanent. It's not a contract. It's a living document that evolves as you do.

Reflection: What would you include in your personal map right now?

- Your anchors:
- Your boundaries:
- Your tools:
- Your values:

The Unexpected Gift

What started as personal understanding has become something I never expected: a way to help others find the same clarity and self-compassion I'd discovered.

When people reach out to share their stories with me, there's a common thread: relief. Not just about having a diagnosis, but about finally having permission to be human. Permission to struggle without it meaning they're broken. Permission to need support without it meaning they're weak.

That's the unexpected gift of understanding your ADHD. It doesn't just change how you see yourself. It changes how you show up in the world.

You become a safer person for other neurodivergent people to be themselves around. You model self-compassion for your kids, your partner, your friends. You show others that it's possible to be human and still be worthy of love.

You give permission for others to stop hiding and start healing. You contribute to a world where being different isn't wrong, it's just different.

When Life Feels Right

Let's get specific about what you're building toward. Not perfection, but alignment.

When life feels right, it might look like:

- Mornings that start gently instead of in a panic
- Work that challenges you without overwhelming you
- Relationships where you can be yourself without performing
- Systems that bend when you need them to
- Recovery time that's built in, not stolen
- Boundaries that protect your energy
- Tools that support instead of complicate
- Conversations where you feel heard and understood
- A pace that feels sustainable, not frantic

This isn't about having everything figured out. It's about having enough figured out that you can navigate with more ease than confusion.

Reflection: When life feels right for you, what does it look like?

The Ongoing Journey

I want to be honest with you: this work doesn't end. Understanding yourself is an ongoing process, not a destination.

Some days you'll feel solid in who you are. Other days you'll catch yourself in old patterns. Both are part of the journey.

The goal isn't to never struggle again. It's to struggle with more awareness, more tools, and more compassion.

You'll keep learning about your brain. You'll keep adjusting your systems. You'll keep growing into who you're becoming.

And that's not a bug. That's a feature.

What's Next

So what comes next? That's up to you.

Maybe you want to dive deeper into specific areas. Maybe you want to focus on one tool and really master it. Maybe you want to take a break and let everything settle.

All of those are valid choices.

The beautiful thing about understanding your brain is that you can trust yourself to know what you need next.

You might need to:

- Practice the tools you've learned
- Share your insights with someone you trust
- Make changes in your environment or relationships
- Seek additional support or resources
- Take time to integrate what you've learned
- Help others who are earlier in their journey

There's no wrong choice. There's only your choice.

Reflection: What would you write in a letter to your future self one year from now?

A Letter to Your Future Self

Before we close, I want you to imagine writing a letter to yourself one year from now.

What would you want that future version of you to know?

Maybe it would sound like this:

"Dear Future Me,

I hope you remember how brave you were to start this journey. I hope you're gentler with yourself than you were a year ago. I hope you've found people who see you clearly and support you fully.

I hope you've learned to trust yourself more. I hope you've built systems that feel sustainable. I hope you've stopped apologizing for being wired differently and started celebrating it.

I hope you remember that progress isn't about perfection. It's about showing up, again and again, with more awareness and compassion each time.

I hope you're proud of how far you've come. And I hope you're excited about where you're going next.

You deserve all the understanding, support, and love you've been afraid to ask for.

With hope and compassion, Your Past Self"

The Final Truth

The final truth I want to leave you with:

You are not a problem to be solved. You are a person to be understood.

Your ADHD isn't something to overcome. It's something to integrate. Your struggles aren't evidence of failure. They're information about what you need.

Your journey doesn't have to look like anyone else's to be valid. Your progress doesn't have to be linear to be real. Your pace doesn't have to be fast to be forward.

You are enough. Right now. As you are. With all your quirks and struggles and beautiful, complicated humanity.

The world needs what you have to offer. Not in spite of your ADHD, but because of how it's shaped your creativity, your empathy, your ability to see patterns others miss, your persistence in the face of challenge.

You've always been enough. Now you're just learning to see it.

One Last Thing

As you close this book and move into whatever comes next, remember this:

You're not graduating from having ADHD. You're graduating to living with it more consciously.

You're not cured. You're equipped.

You're not fixed. You're informed.

You're not starting over. You're starting with the right map.

And that map? It's going to take you places you never imagined possible.

Understanding your brain doesn't eliminate challenges, it transforms how you approach them. It changes you from someone who fights their own operating system to someone who works with it. From someone who apologizes for their differences to someone who leverages them. From someone who hides their struggles to someone who uses them as information.

Welcome to the rest of your life. It's going to be different from what you expected.

It's going to be better.

This isn't the end. It's the beginning. You have everything you need to keep growing, learning, and becoming more fully yourself.

The journey continues. And you're exactly where you need to be.

Sidenote: This journey of understanding and integration continues throughout your life. You might discover additional aspects of neurodivergence, develop new tools, or find that your needs change over time. That's not backsliding, that's growth. Stay curious about yourself and open to what you might learn next.

Key takeaways: You're not starting over. You're starting with the right map. Progress isn't linear, and it doesn't have to be fast to be forward. You are not a problem to be solved; you are a person to be understood. The world needs what you have to offer, not in spite of your ADHD, but because of how it's shaped your creativity, empathy, and resilience.

About the Author

Tyler Mitchell is a strategy consultant, content creator, and ADHD advocate who has transformed his late-in-life diagnosis into a mission to help others navigate neurodivergence with clarity and compassion. Through his viral social media content and comprehensive guides, he's helped tens of thousands of people understand their ADHD brains and build systems that actually work.

Diagnosed with ADHD in his 40s after researching for his neurodivergent son, Tyler brings both lived experience and analytical expertise to the conversation. As a father of five (with multiple neurodivergent family members), homeschool educator, and business professional, he understands the real-world challenges of managing ADHD across all areas of life.

Tyler's authentic approach to ADHD advocacy has resonated widely. His content has been viewed millions of times. His interactive guides have helped hundreds of adults build sustainable systems for work, parenting, and daily life.

When he's not creating content or consulting on strategy projects, Tyler can be found pacing while thinking (his preferred method), having deep conversations with his kids about neurodivergence, or reorganizing his entire productivity system for the 47th time.

Resources

For Deeper Implementation:

This book focuses on the personal journey and stories of living with ADHD after diagnosis. For comprehensive tools, exercises, and systematic implementation:

"So You Were Diagnosed with ADHD, Now What? - Complete Guide" at store.tylermitchell.com includes:

- 10-Chapter Interactive Framework with detailed exercises
- Practical tools and experiments to try with your brain
- Notion Template Workspace for tracking what works
- Self-directed learning at your own pace

Use code BOOKBONUS for 20% off.

Additional specialized guides covering work, family, and other specific areas of ADHD life are also available at store.tylermitchell.com.

Books for Further Reading:

- "Driven to Distraction" by Edward Hallowell
- "The ADHD Effect on Marriage" by Melissa Orlov
- "Taking Charge of Adult ADHD" by Russell Barkley

Organizations:

- CHADD (Children and Adults with ADHD): chadd.org
- ADDA (Attention Deficit Disorder Association): add.org
- ADDitude Magazine: additudemag.com

Professional Support:

- Psychology Today therapist directory
- ADHD Coaches Organization
- Your primary care physician for medication discussions

Online Communities:

- Reddit: r/ADHD, r/ADHDers
- Facebook: Various ADHD support groups

Resources

- TikTok: #ADHDtok community

For Ongoing Support:

Visit tylermitchell.com for:

- Regular content updates
- Community discussions
- New tools and insights as I continue learning

Quick Reference Guide

Key Concepts from This Book

ADHD Pendulum: The swing between "on fire" (hyperfocused, overcommitted) and "burned out" (exhausted, shut down) modes. Natural for many people with ADHD.

Attention-Emotion-Energy Triangle: ADHD affects all three simultaneously. When one is off, the others follow.

Body Doubling: Having another person present while you work. They don't have to help or watch - just being there helps many ADHD brains focus.

Masking: Copying what seems "normal" in social situations for safety, often at the cost of authenticity and energy.

Rejection Sensitive Dysphoria (RSD): Intense emotional reaction to perceived rejection or criticism, common in ADHD.

Reset Anchors: Small, concrete actions that help you regulate when swinging too far toward overwhelm or burnout.

Time Blindness: Difficulty accurately perceiving the passage of time. Minutes can feel like hours or hours can disappear.

Working Memory: Your brain's "scratchpad" that holds information while you use it. Often glitchy in ADHD.

Key Reframes
- **Old:** "I'm inconsistent"
  New: "I'm cyclical"
- **Old:** "I'm easily distracted"
  New: "I have trouble controlling where my focus goes"
- **Old:** "I'm too emotional"
  New: "I experience emotions intensely"

- **Old:** "I can't handle normal life"
  New: "I'm managing invisible cognitive load"
- **Old:** "I'm making excuses"
  New: "I'm advocating for what I need"

The One-Box System

When overwhelmed, organize your day into three categories:

- **What matters most:** The one thing that would make today feel worthwhile
- **What needs done:** Essential tasks that must happen
- **What I'll forgive:** Things that can wait without guilt

Common ADHD Patterns

Amazon Delivery Loop: Stress/boredom → online shopping → guilt → productivity pressure → overwhelm → repeat

Perfect System Paradox: Frustration → research new system → excitement → works briefly → feels restrictive → abandon → repeat

Overcommit Cycle: Excitement → say yes to everything → realize overload → panic → burn out → guilt → repeat

---

Terms You Might Encounter

Neurotypical: Someone whose brain development and functioning is considered "typical" by medical and social standards.

Neurodivergent: Having a brain that functions differently from what's considered neurotypical. Includes ADHD, autism, dyslexia, and others.

Executive Function: The brain's management system that handles planning, organizing, initiating tasks, and switching between activities.

Hyperfocus: Intense concentration on something interesting, often to the exclusion of everything else.

Stimming: Self-regulating repetitive behaviors like fidgeting, leg bouncing, or pen clicking. Helps with focus and emotional regulation.

Comorbid/Comorbidity: Having multiple conditions at the same time (like ADHD and anxiety).

Accommodations: Changes to environment or approach that help someone function better (like noise-canceling headphones or written instructions).

Interoception: Your ability to sense internal body signals like hunger, fatigue, or emotional states.

Task Initiation: The ability to start activities or tasks. Often challenging for people with ADHD.

Dopamine: A brain chemical involved in motivation, reward, and attention. Often dysregulated in ADHD.

Emergency Strategies

When Overwhelmed:

- Name three things you can see, hear, and feel
- Take 5 deep breaths
- Ask: "What would I do if I only had energy for one thing?"

When Stuck/Can't Start:

- Set a 10-minute timer and commit to just beginning
- Change your environment (different room, music, lighting)
- Find someone to body double with

When Spiraling:

- Remember: This feeling is temporary
- Reach out to someone who understands
- Use a reset anchor from your toolkit

When Burned Out:

- Lower expectations to match actual capacity
- Focus on basics: sleep, food, gentle movement
- Remind yourself: Rest is productive

Quick Disclosure Scripts

Simple: "I have ADHD, which means my brain processes things differently sometimes."

Workplace: "I work better with clear expectations, deadlines and regular check-ins."

Social: "I might need things repeated or written down - it helps me process better."

Boundary: "I'm not looking for advice, just wanted to share where I'm at."

A Guide for Partners, Family & Friends

How to support someone with ADHD

If someone you care about has shared their ADHD diagnosis with you, thank you for wanting to understand. This section will help you support them more effectively.

What ADHD Actually Is

ADHD isn't about being lazy, unmotivated, or "not trying hard enough." It's a neurological difference that affects:

- **Attention regulation** (they can't always control what they focus on)
- **Emotional processing** (feelings can be more intense)
- **Executive function** (planning, organizing, starting tasks)
- **Time perception** (minutes can feel like hours, hours can disappear)
- **Working memory** (forgetting things mid-conversation or mid-task)

What You Might Notice

They might:

- Seem scattered or forgetful, then hyperfocus for hours on something random
- Get overwhelmed by things that seem simple to you
- Need more time to process information or instructions
- Have intense emotional reactions to small setbacks
- Struggle with time management despite really caring about being on time
- Start many projects but finish few
- Need to move, fidget, or pace while thinking

This isn't personal. It's not about you or how much they care. It's about how their brain works.

How to Help

Communication

- **Be specific** rather than vague ("Please take out the trash tonight" vs. "Help with chores")
- **Write things down** when possible, especially if there are multi-step instructions
- **Check for understanding** without being patronizing ("Should I send you a recap email?")
- **Be patient with questions** - they might need clarification, not because they weren't listening

Emotional Support

- **Don't minimize their struggles** ("Everyone forgets things sometimes")
- **Avoid "helpful" suggestions** unless asked ("Have you tried making a list?")
- **Recognize their effort** - they're often working twice as hard as it appears
- **Stay calm during emotional moments** - their intensity isn't about you

Practical Support

- **Help with systems, not judgment** ("What would make this easier?" vs. "You should be more organized")
- **Respect their accommodations** (earplugs, fidget toys, need for movement)
- **Understand their rhythms** - they might need recovery time after social events or busy periods
- **Be flexible with plans** - their energy and capacity can fluctuate unexpectedly

What NOT to Say

"You don't look/act like you have ADHD"
"Everyone has trouble focusing sometimes"
"You just need more discipline"
"Have you tried just writing it down?"
"You're using ADHD as an excuse"
"You were fine before you got diagnosed"

What TO Say

✓ "How can I best support you with this?"
✓ "That sounds really challenging"
✓ "What do you need from me right now?"
✓ "I'm still learning - can you help me understand?"
✓ "I appreciate you sharing this with me"
✓ "You're doing the best you can"

Understanding Their Struggles

Time and Planning

They're not being disrespectful when they're late. Time perception is genuinely different for many people with ADHD. They might:

- Underestimate how long things take
- Get distracted during transitions
- Struggle with prioritizing preparation steps

How to help: Build in buffer time, send gentle reminders, help them identify what derails their routine.

Emotional Intensity

Small criticisms might trigger big reactions (rejection sensitive dysphoria). They're not being dramatic - their brain processes rejection as genuine threat.

How to help: Frame feedback positively, give them time to process, reassure them of your relationship.

The Pendulum Swing

They might go from "crushing everything" to "can't reply to a text" seemingly overnight. This is natural ADHD cycling, not personal inconsistency.

How to help: Don't take their low periods personally, help them plan for recovery time, celebrate their high-energy contributions.

Supporting Without Enabling

There's a difference between supporting someone with ADHD and doing everything for them:

Support: "What system would help you remember this?"
Enabling: Always remembering everything for them

Support: "How can we make mornings less stressful?"
Enabling: Doing all their morning tasks for them

Support: "What do you need to focus on this project?"
Enabling: Doing the project for they

The goal is helping them build systems that work, not becoming their external executive function.

Taking Care of Yourself

Supporting someone with ADHD can be exhausting, especially if you're naturally organized or neurotypical. Remember:

- **Set your own boundaries** - you can't regulate their emotions for them
- Don't take their struggles personally - their bad days aren't about you
- **Seek your own support** if needed - ADHD impacts the whole family system
- Celebrate progress, not perfection – even small improvements matter

When to Encourage Professional Help

Encourage them to seek additional support if:

- They continue to struggle with daily functioning despite having strategies in place
- Their emotional regulation seems to be getting worse
- They're having thoughts of self-harm
- Relationship or work problems are escalating
- They want to explore medication or therapy options

Remember

Your person with ADHD has likely spent years feeling "broken" or "not enough." Your understanding, patience, and genuine support can make an enormous difference in their healing journey.

They're not asking you to fix them - they're asking you to see them clearly and love them as they are, ADHD and all.

Learn More

If you want to understand ADHD better:

- Read this book yourself
- Follow reputable ADHD educators online
- Couples/family therapy with an ADHD-informed therapist
- Join support communities for ADHD families

Your willingness to learn means everything.

www.ingramcontent.com/pod-product-compliance
Lightning Source LLC
Chambersburg PA
CBHW051633120626
46551CB00014B/2058